SCENE ONE

Sketches for church drama groups

by

ASHLEY MARTIN, ANDY KELSO
AND OTHERS

KINGSWAY PUBLICATIONS
EASTBOURNE

First published 1986

ISBN 0 86065 325 0

Front cover illustration: Vic Mitchell

Printed in Great Britain for
KINGSWAY PUBLICATIONS LTD
Lottbridge Drove, Eastbourne, E. Sussex BN23 6NT by
Cox & Wyman Ltd, Reading
Typeset by Nuprint Services, Harpenden, Herts.

Contents

Performing Licence

If you wish to perform any of the pieces in this book, you are free to do so without charge provided the performance is in the context of worship or evangelistic outreach. The purchase of this book constitutes a licence granting the right to perform the sketches in such amateur contexts.

This will not give you permission to reproduce the text in any way; permission to do this must be sought from the publishers (see copyright notice at the front of the book).

Those engaging in commercial performances should make a separate approach to the appropriate author (addresses listed below), as this will involve the payment of royalties on box office takings.

All film, video and audio recording rights of pieces that appear in Sections 1 and 2 are reserved by the publishers.

Ashley Martin, 12 Abbotsbury, Orton Malborne, Peterborough, Cambridgeshire PE2 OPS.

Andy Kelso, 37 Hanley Avenue, Old Bramcote, Nottingham.

John Fewings, 13 Eden Drive, St. Andrews Way, Hull, North Humberside.

Stuart Todd, 49 Kingsley Avenue, Hartlepool, Cleveland.

Pamela Ive, Pheasants Lodge, 6 Bracken View, Brocton, Stafford ST17 OTF.

John Beattie, 12 Pirbright Road, Farnborough, Hampshire GU14 7AD.

Roland Heaney, 15 St John's Park, Belfast BT7 3JF, N. Ireland.

Graeme Kent, White Lodge, 43 Dilleys Lane, Boston, Lincolnshire.

Adrian Self, 38 Paragon, Bath, Avon.

Stage Directions

The stage directions used in this book are the conventional ones (see below). They come from a time when troupes of actors toured the country in carts. The side of the cart was let down to form a stage. As this stage had a slope, or rake, to be near to the audience was thus *down*stage, and conversely the back of the stage was *up*. Left and Right are always taken from the actors' standpoint when facing the audience.

These directions may be taken merely as a rough guide to positioning since acting areas vary so much in shape, size and height. For this reason, an actor should always pay careful attention to where his audience are and how much they can see. If you are performing on the same level as a flat-seated audience, anyone beyond the second row will only see your head at best. Compensations should be made if the piece requires you to kneel or sit at any time. Also, entrances should be timed according to the length of time it takes to get onto a particular stage. Although it may only be a step or two more than last time the piece was performed, it could make all the difference, especially if tight rhythm is being used. *Always* rehearse in a new space.

KEY

U = UP   M = MID   L = LEFT   C = CENTRE
D = DOWN   O = OFF   R = RIGHT   S = STAGE

The letters are also used in other combinations not included in the diagram; thus SL = Stage left, DS = down stage, and so on.

Foreword

Drama in church? Surely this is a gimmick....

Well, it can be. Anything done simply for effect can be a gimmick. But ask yourself if Old Testament prophets like Jeremiah or Ezekiel, or New Testament characters like Agabus, despised the medium of drama. Our Lord himself did not merely speak: he acted. He embodied his message in flesh, and the supreme events of the incarnation, atonement and resurrection were all *enacted*. It is hardly surprising, therefore, that drama remains a most powerful medium of communication. It is one of the ways God himself has sanctioned and used to the full.

There is, therefore, no reason why drama should not be part of our offering to God in worship. There is nothing new about it either. In the Middle Ages, for instance, the truths of the Christian faith were often portrayed in mime and mystery plays. And today in many parts of the church there is a desire to give dramatic expression to the faith. But where are the scripts? This has been the problem.

The same applies to evangelism. Drama is exceedingly powerful in missions, as I thankfully acknowledge. It can often communicate at a depth where preaching alone does not penetrate. I have used it not only in set pieces in town halls, student unions and parish churches, but in open air as well—in the streets and market places of our towns and cities. And always it provokes interest, always it draws a crowd, always it facilitates conversation about the Lord.

The need for drama scripts in worship and evangelism has been paramount for some time. The trouble has been that very few combine the necessary professional skills with the Christian commitment to provide such scripts. But that is precisely what these authors provide.

As you will see, the book contains three main sections. There are the short, punchy scripts of Ashley Martin. There are the longer scripts of my good friend Andy Kelso, a most talented actor and until recently, head of the Christian Arts Centre in London. And there are the scripts of the seven finalists of the Buzz/Kingsway sketch-writing competition. Here is a variety of material for use in many different situations. Christian groups are crying out for scripts like these, and I am delighted that Kingsway is making them widely available.

When Billy Graham came to do a short mission in the University of Oxford, he wanted to take our Christian drama team away with him because he realized the additional impact it provided to his preaching. Drama can often get through to people who are resistant to preaching. I sometimes use one or more dramatic sketches in the middle of a mission address, and it is very effective.

I have great pleasure in commending this book to the public, and my hope is that the sketches will not only bring illumination and freshness of impact wherever they are used, but that they will stimulate people with dramatic talent (and even more who think they have none) to use that gift for the service of Christ.

Canon Michael Green,
St Aldate's Rectory,
Oxford

SECTION 1

by

Ashley Martin

A Word from the Author

God is alive!

God is not only alive, but he is very active, and is still seeking a relationship with each one of us today. This is the starting point and the central theme of each of these sketches. Each sketch takes a look at the relationship of individuals with God, and at their responses to his plan for their lives.

The Bible from start to finish is full of action and drama. Throughout the Bible we see God initiating and man responding; God commanding, and man obeying or choosing to disobey; God speaking, and man listening or choosing not to listen. What more dramatic beginning could there be than the creation of the universe, and what more dramatic climax than the return of the risen Son of God to claim those whom he himself has redeemed and fashioned to be his perfect bride? And throughout the whole story it is God who remains centre stage.

Of course it is impossible to declare the whole counsel of God in one sketch, just as it is in one sermon, one article, poem or song. Each of these sketches is a short illustration, depicting a small fragment of what it means to know, serve and follow God. I hope they will be useful in helping to illuminate and bring to life something of what God is saying to us today. I hope too that they will help those of you who have found and received the gift of life to share that life with others.

Many of these sketches were pioneered by the Christian Union Drama Group at Lancaster University during my time there from 1978 to 1982. I remain indebted to them for all their hard work and encouragement.

The Bible tells us we are made in the image of God. Our Creator made us to be creative, but only when our creativity is established on firm godly foundations can it fulfil its true potential. At a conference I once attended one of the speakers put it something like this: skill and creativity are very important, and if we are to truly glorify God in our creative ministries, it is vital to pursue skilfulness and excellence. But skill and creativity without a worshipping spirit and submission to God are nothing more than clanging cymbals.

I hope that the sketches in this book will encourage you to generate your own ideas and sketches, to experiment and develop new ways of expressing your love for God, and God's love and commitment to man. I hope, too, that you will have a great deal of fun and enjoyment in rehearsing and performing them. It is my prayer that the God who created the heavens and the earth should be at the heart of our creativeness, and that in our lives and performances he should always remain centre stage.

Ashley Martin

The publishers are grateful for the editorial help of Philip Hawthorn, artistic director of Primary Colours Mime Theatre, in the final presentation of these sketches.

Beyond Belief

A sketch about obedience to God, no matter how ridiculous the instructions seem and what others think. Also how we reduce God to our human ways of thinking, forgetting his limitless power.

CHARACTERS: JOSH
RACHEL
ZEB
REUBEN

(Any part can be played by either sex, with appropriate name change.)

(Note: NOAH *is imagined on top of a hill OSL (see stage key).)*

SCENE: *An empty stage.* JOSH, RACHEL *and* ZEB *enter SL talking.* REUBEN *lags behind.* JOSH *looks USL, sees something and turns to face DS and stops.* OTHERS *bump into him and also stop SC, looking DS.*

ZEB: What's up Josh?

JOSH: Ssshh! Don't look now, but look what's happening behind us.

*(*OTHERS *look puzzled, trying to work out* JOSH*'s instructions.)*

REUBEN: *(turning to look)* What's he—

JOSH: *(pulling him round)* I said don't look. Act nonchalant.

*(*ALL *twiddle thumbs, whistle and turn around slowly.* REUBEN *stays staring at the hill. Others pull him to face DS.)*

RACHEL: What's he building?

JOSH: Beats me.

ZEB: It's obvious, ain't it? *(*OTHERS *stare at him.)* Well...it's a...he's making a...you know! *(*OTHERS *shake their heads)*...*you* know...it's a... *(turns quickly and views hill from several angles.)*

JOSH: *(pulling him round)* He'll see us!

RACHEL: So what. We're friends of his, aren't we?

ZEB: Yeah, what difference does it make?

JOSH: It may be a secret. *(*OTHERS *laugh.)*

RACHEL: It can't be a secret, that big! It's nearly as big as the hill he's building it on—whatever it is.

REUBEN: My left knee's hurting. *(*OTHERS *stop and stare at* REUBEN.*)* It means trouble, you mark my words—my left knee's always right.

ZEB: I thought you walked funny.

(All except REUBEN *laugh, then stop abruptly as if they hear their names called.)*

JOSH: Ssshh! Leave this to me, act natural. *(Turns to face SL.)* Oh, hello Noah, fancy seeing you here. *(Listens.)* Oh nothing—just passing. Lovely weather, eh? Could do with a bit of rain for my dahlias though.

ZEB: *(turning SL)* Ask him what he's—

JOSH: *(shoving him back, still looking SL. Whispering loudly.)* Leave this to *me*. We were just admiring your...er...what is it exactly? *(Listens.)* Oh.

REUBEN: It means no good.

JOSH: Yes, thanks. *(Turns to* OTHERS.*)*

ZEB: What did he say then?

JOSH: He says he's building an ark.

RACHEL: An ark?

ZEB: Oh, an ark. What's an ark?

REUBEN: *(aside)* Part of a circle.

JOSH: Well it's a... *(turns SL.)* Noah! Hello, yes, er, what *is* an ark? *(Listens.)*

REUBEN: *(suspiciously)* What does he want with part of a circle? Perhaps it's a sign of doom.

RACHEL: Oh shut up, you old misery.

JOSH: *(finishing conversation.)* OK, thanks. *(Turns back.)*

OTHERS: Well?

JOSH: He says he's building something for his family to live in.

RACHEL: What, a house?

JOSH: No...a massive boat—he's building a massive boat *(pause)* on top of a hill. *(Slowly starts to giggle in short bursts.*

OTHERS *look at him and gradually join in. The whole impression should be of trying not to let* NOAH *notice them laughing.)*

(Controlling himself.) Excuse me again Noah. Forgive me asking, but *why* are you building a big boat to live in—what's wrong with a tent? *(Listens.)*

RACHEL: Always was a bit funny, old Noah.

ZEB: *(sarcastically)* Tents aren't good enough for him!

REUBEN: I still don't like it.

JOSH: Oh. *(Turns, smirking.)* He says it's 'cos tents are easily flooded...on top of a hill. *(Giggles again.) (Turning.)* But Noah, you're miles from any water—eh? you what? *(over shoulder to* OTHERS.*)* Here, get this, he says it's going to rain. *(Turns back to* NOAH.*)*

RACHEL: But it hasn't rained for months.

ZEB: Years.

REUBEN: Mind you, he could be right, my shoulder's playing up. Always plays up in bad weather.

RACHEL: And good weather, and any time there's work to be done.

JOSH: *(over shoulder)* Sssh! *(To* NOAH*)* How do you know it's going to rain? *(Listens.)* Oh. *(Turns DS.)* God told him. *(Chuckles—turns back.* OTHERS *groan.)*

ZEB: Not God again.

RACHEL: Religious nutty Noah—him and his God.

REUBEN: Our God too.

ZEB: *(laughing)* Here, I bet God told him to build the ark.

JOSH: *(turning DS)* And God told him to build the ark. *(All laugh.)* Eh? *(Turns back to* NOAH, *biting his lip.)* Oh...yeah. *(Turns DS.)* He says God's not pleased with the way men have *(turns to* OTHERS *SR)* turned their backs on him, filling the world with evil and violence—so he's going to wash it all away and start again wth those kept safe in the boat.

ZEB: *(indicating Noah)* 'Ark at 'im *(All laugh except* REUBEN.*)*

REUBEN: I knew it, we're all doomed—the end is at hand.

ZEB: Shut up Reuben!

JOSH: *(turning SL)* Now look, Noah—aren't you taking all this a bit far? *(Placating.)* All right! All right! I'm just worried for you—do you know what people are saying about you? *(ZEB and RACHEL whisper and giggle)* What do you mean you don't care? Listen—yes... I know you said it was the voice of God—but if everyone went around saying 'God said this, God said that' where would we be?

RACHEL: You tell him, Josh.

REUBEN: Doomed! We're all going to die.

ZEB & RACHEL: Shut up!

JOSH: Listen Noah—think about it logically, rationally, like any other human being—eh? What do you mean that's typical of us limiting God to the realms of human logic?

ZEB: What's logic?

RACHEL: Oh use your common sense.

JOSH: Anyway, that thing's far too big for you and your family. *(Listens)* Animals? but you haven't got any pets. Eh? You're joking. *(Turns.)* He's going to take two of every kind of animal in the world! *(They all laugh, except REUBEN who is looking at the sky.)*

(Regaining composure.) OK Noah, you've had your joke—come down and we'll go and have a drink. No? What? Look, I'm just about getting to the end of my—

ZEB: *(noticing something SR)* Look! *(ALL look SR.)* Animals.

RACHEL: *(Quietly)* Hundreds of 'em.

JOSH: Thousands.

REUBEN: The end is nigh! *(Their heads follow the animals from USR to USL, then up to the ark.)*

JOSH: It's a public liability, a health hazard *(Shouting.)* You should put those leopards on leads—and—

RACHEL: It's an insult, Noah—that great thing's dangerous.

ZEB: I bet you haven't got planning permission.

REUBEN: *(still looking up)* Won't be long now—look at those grey clouds—we're doomed.

OTHERS: No we're not!

JOSH: *(to REUBEN)* Look, if you're so sure you're right, why don't you go and live with Noah. You'll love all those bears, tigers, snakes and spiders. *(REUBEN looks more and more sheepish, looks up, looks at the ark.)*

REUBEN: On the other hand, I could be wrong.

(OTHERS laugh. REUBEN eventually joins in.)

JOSH: He's mad I tell you—eh? *(To* NOAH*)* What do you mean, 'Everything's gone to the dogs'?

ZEB: The dogs have gone to Noah! *(*ALL *laugh.)*

JOSH: *(to* NOAH*)* Eh?—no-one's happy with things the way they are? We're happy enough. *(*ALL *laugh, slapping each other.)*

RACHEL: *(mimicking)* God told me to! *(Laughter.)*

ZEB: God's a weather forecaster! *(Laughter.)*

JOSH: The meteor-illogical office! *(*ALL *roll around on the floor.)*

(As they laugh, they start to beat the floor with their fists. Eventually the laughter dies away, and the fists become palms, the slapping is the sound of rain. This gets louder. All look up, worried. (If possible) a thunder clap is heard.)

ALL *freeze.*

Stiff-Necked People

A piece about disobedience and unbelief. Mainly for Christians, to illustrate God's greatness and faithfulness and man's fickleness.

CHARACTERS: FIRST ISRAELITE
SECOND ISRAELITE
CROWD—minimum of four
MOSES

During the piece, CROWD *form a tennis crowd group between* 1ST *and* 2ND ISRAELITES *and* MOSES. CROWD *should look at the speaker wherever possible—in unison.*

SCENE: *The Israelites have just crossed the Red Sea and escaped from the Egyptians. There is a sign MSL, pointing SL, reading: 'RED SEA ½ MILE. NO BRIDGE.'*

Loud cheers are heard OSL. Enter 1ST ISRAELITE, *goes to sign, reads it, takes out pen and writes, 'Who needs one?' underneath. Enter* CROWD *SL talking excitedly. They assemble USC.*

1ST ISRAELITE: Hey, we've made it! *(Moves DSR.)*

CROWD: We've made it!

2ND ISRAELITE: *(entering SL)* The Egyptians can't get us now, we're free. *(Moves DSR.)*

CROWD: We're free!

1ST IS: A miracle, we're safe!

CROWD: We're safe!

MOSES: *(Entering SL, stands MSL)* Thanks be to God who has surely saved us.

CROWD: The Lord has triumphed, thanks be to God!

MOSES: He has defeated our enemies, we will always praise him.

CROWD: We will always praise him!

1ST IS: Hey, wait a minute, I'm starving.

CROWD: *(still cheering)* I'm starving!

1ST IS: No, listen—we've no food.

CROWD: No food! *(Realizing.)* No food? *(Panic.)* No food! What are we going to do? *(Etc.)*

2ND IS: We'll starve.

CROWD: We'll starve, we'll starve—help!

1ST IS: Moses, why have you done this to us? If only we were in Egypt now. Lots of food in Egypt.

2ND IS: Don't let us die here, take us back to Egypt.

CROWD: Yes, take us back to Egypt.

MOSES: Stop! *(CROWD are silent.)* It's not me you're murmuring against, but God. He has saved you from slavery and yet you still won't listen and trust him. He will provide you with food to eat.

CROWD: How can he provide us with food? There's none to be seen.

1ST IS: *(noticing something OSR)* Look, food!

CROWD: *(looking in all directions)* Where?

1ST IS: There! *(CROWD look OSR in unison on a beat.)* Raining down from heaven, enough for all of us.

CROWD: *(heads centre, hands praising)* There is food. Oh the Lord is great, the Lord provides. He has given us bread to eat. He will always provide. We will always follow him.

2ND IS: Hey, wait a minute.

CROWD: *(heads SR)* What?

2ND IS: Nothing to drink!

CROWD: *(hands down, heads centre)* Nothing to drink! We've nothing to drink! We'll die of thirst!

1ST IS: Is the Lord among us or not?

2ND IS: Lots to drink back in Egypt.

CROWD: *(heads centre)* Oh to be in Egypt again, now that spring is here—take us back to Egypt.

MOSES: Why do you find fault? Has not God proved his love for you? Just as he provided bread for you, so will he provide water.

CROWD: *(heads centre)* Water, water, give us water!

1ST IS: *(noticing OSL)* Look, water!

CROWD: Where? *(Heads turn SL, centre.)* Water! We are saved!

2ND IS: Now we know the Lord's greatness.

CROWD: *(hands raised)* The Lord is faithful, the Lord is triumphant. We will always serve the Lord.

MOSES: And will you serve God alone, and no other gods?

CROWD: We will, we will.

MOSES: And will you make no graven images?

CROWD: We will make no...er...What?

MOSES: Graven images.

CROWD: None of them!

MOSES *exits SR. The* CROWD *talk among themselves of God's greatness.* 1ST IS *breaks away and looks into the distance OSR.*

2ND IS: Where's Moses gone?

1ST IS: Up to Mount Sinai.

CROWD: *(heads SR, heads angle up)* That's miles away.

2ND IS: He might never come back. It's the last we've seen of him. Some leader!

CROWD: *(alarmed, heads centre)* Some leader! What shall we do?

1ST IS: Well, we'd better do something.

CROWD: *(in unison put chins on hands)* Errrm.

2ND IS: I know. *(*CROWD *looks)* Let's make gods who will go before us.

CROWD: Yes, let's make gods.

1ST and 2ND IS: Let us make—*(Pause.)* A golden calf.

ALL: *(hands raise)* Praise to the golden calf!

*(*ALL *freeze.)*

The Wall

A piece about obedience and how God honours it. Also, how his ways are definitely not ours.

People do not always have to play people. The tree of Zacchaeus, Jonah's conscience—these can be 'characters' too. It is also an idea to approach stories from a different angle. How did the wall of Jericho react to the Israelites' invasion?

CHARACTERS: WALL—Three people on chairs, backs to audience with 'wall drape' around their shoulders. Plus one to be voice of WALL.
CHRIS—A stranger outside the city. Can be male or female.
LEADER—ie. of ISRAELITES.
ISRAELITES—Minimum of three.

SCENE: *Outside Jericho.* WALL *stands MSC.*
Enter CHRIS *SR shaking paint spray can. Goes to spray the* WALL *when* ISRAELITES *enter SL and march past.* CHRIS *hides can and pretends nothing is going on.* ISRAELITES *exit SR.* CHRIS *takes off lid and after a careful look around, goes to spray* WALL.

WALL: Oi! *(*CHRIS *jumps and looks around.)*
CHRIS: Who said that?
WALL: Me!
CHRIS: Who, I can't see anyone?
WALL: Here, behind you.
CHRIS: A wall? A wall that talks?
WALL: Well, we're supposed to have ears so we may as well have mouths as well. Hey, you weren't thinking of spraying that on me were you?

CHRIS: Oh...er...no! It's, er, my deodorant, yeah *(sniffs armpit)* Phaw! *(Makes noise of spraying.)* Ah, that's better. Hey, you're a nice wall, strong. *(CHRIS talks to the wall, but never turns more US than SL.)*

WALL: Indestructible mate, in-de-struct-i-ble.

CHRIS: Yeah, bet you can't be knocked down either. Where am I anyway?

WALL: Jericho, isn't it—one of the principal cities in Canaan, with its famed fortitudinous fortifications.

CHRIS: You what?

WALL: Strong wall.

CHRIS: Oh yeah.

(ISRAELITES enter SR, DS of CHRIS. They march past. CHRIS nods politely, ISRAELITES exit SL.)

Hey, is that the guard?

WALL: What? You must be joking—that lot couldn't guard a fire. They've been marching round here for days—they're a bunch of wallies if you ask me.

CHRIS: Wallies? Don't you mean wall-ies. *(Laughs.)* Get it? *(WALL gives no response)* Oh never mind.

(Enter ISRAELITES SL.)

(Runs to the LEADER.) 'Scuse me.

LEADER: *(not stopping)* What.

CHRIS: *(keeping up)* What are you doing?

LEADER: *(stopping)* What does it look like?

CHRIS: Marching round a wall.

LEADER: Right. *(Starts marching.)*

CHRIS: *(following)* Why?

LEADER: *(stopping)* Orders, that's why—any more questions?

CHRIS: Yeah, why are you ordered to walk round it?

LEADER: It's a military manoeuvre.

WALL: But the wall—...er someone said that you weren't guarding him—it.

LEADER: That's because we're not, we are the attack. We are demolishing it.

(WALL laughs.)

LEADER: Pardon?

CHRIS: *(coughing)* Nothing. You've, er, not actually got very far, have you?

LEADER: We've nearly finished.

CHRIS: *(WALL laughs again, CHRIS grins)* Oh, that's a good 'un, nearly finished. Very good, very funny indeed.

LEADER: *(a little exasperated)* Look, you smart alec. Any minute now this 'ere wall is going to come tumbling down, and if you're not careful, you'll end up in the rubble.

CHRIS: But you haven't even started hacking away at it yet. Anyway, you could never knock that wall down. It's too strong.

WALL: You bet your camel.

LEADER: We're not going to knock it down, it's going to fall down. We're just following orders.

CHRIS: Whose orders?

LEADER: God's orders, that's who.

(WALL laughs and shakes.)

CHRIS: Come on, stop mucking around. Who really put you up to this?

LEADER: I've already told you.

CHRIS: *(incredulously)* You mean—you're serious? You expect this God of yours to knock this wall down just because you've marched round it a few times?

WALL: I told you they were wallies.

LEADER: He isn't just any god you know. He is God, the Lord, the Almighty.

CHRIS: Well, that's as maybe. But I still say that nothing could knock this wall down.

LEADER: Look. If our God is capable of getting us across the Red Sea and over the Jordan without us getting our feet wet, I hardly think this wall here is going to give him a lot of trouble.

WALL: I'll give you trouble, mate.

CHRIS: *(sarcastically)* OK, so when you finish marching up and down, what do you do then?

LEADER: We blow our trumpets.

CHRIS: *(laughing)* You what?

LEADER: We blow our trumpets and make a lot of noise.

CHRIS and WALL: *(laughing)* You're off your rocker.

CHRIS: Sun must 'ave got to them. After all, they have been marching round this city all day.

LEADER: Six days actually. Anyway, I can't stand here gossiping to you all day. It's nearly time to invade.

WALL: He really believes it doesn't he?

LEADER: If God says it's going to happen, that's good enough for me. Stand back, please.

CHRIS: *(shrugging his shoulders and moving away)* Absolute nutter. That wall will never…

(As the ISRAELITES *shout and blow their trumpets, there is a loud rumble.* CHRIS *turns and looks in amazement, as* WALL *shakes and collapses. They freeze. A voice is heard from off stage.)*

VOICE: Oi. You can't do that to our wall!

Whom Shall I Send?

A sketch about God's calling each one of us to fulfil our own individual tasks as part of his plan. The sketch demands slick timing of moves and words so that the flow is not lost. Quite often actors are required to talk as they move into position. The mood changes dramatically from the light-hearted accounts of the calls of Moses and Jonah, to the more serious account of Jesus' commission. Thus, the rhythm slows down. Perhaps most useful as a challenge to Christians, but not entirely limited to this sphere.

CHARACTERS: GOD
1/SAILOR
2/JONAH
3/MOSES/SAILOR
4/CHORUS
5/JESUS

Empty stage except for a chair USC. Enter GOD, *stands on chair, faces us. Enter* 1, 2, *speaking as they move to MSC—one each side of chair.)*

1: The Lord came down to Moses.
2: The Lord said *(Both look at* GOD.*)*
GOD: *(turning)* I have a task for you.
1: And Moses said:
3/MOSES: *(entering SL)* Here I am, Lord, *(Moves DSL.)*
4: *(entering)* Please. *(Stays SL.)*
3/MOSES: Send someone else. *(Faces audience.)*
5: *(entering)* He said: *(Stays SL.)*
3/MOSES: I don't know who to say has sent me.
1: And the Lord said:
GOD: I AM.
2: And Moses said:
3/MOSES: Pardon? *(Turns to face* GOD.*)*
4: And God said:
GOD: I am who I am. Tell the people that I am the Lord God of your fathers and have sent you to bring them out of Egypt.
5: But Moses wasn't happy. He said:
3/MOSES: I'm not happy.
4: He said:
3/MOSES: They won't listen to me.
1, 2, 4, 5: Yes they will.
3/MOSES: No they won't.
4: And God said:
GOD: I will give you signs and wonders, miracles to perform. Then they will believe.
1, 5: Then Moses was happy.
3/MOSES: No I'm not!
1, 2, 4, 5: Why?
GOD: Why?
2: And Moses said:
3/MOSES: O Lord, I am not eloquent. I have not the words. *(Turns to audience.)* I am not possessive of the linguistic capability and the powers of oration with which to purvey the message so graciously entrusted to me in a manner which would convince the recipients of the efficacy of

what I am say—

5: O shut up!

3/MOSES: You see?

4: And God said:

GOD: Who made man to speak? Who made him deaf or dumb, seeing or blind? Is it not I? Go, and I will speak through you.

1: And Moses said:

3/MOSES: But—

2: And the Lord said:

GOD: *(resigned)* Oh, very well. Take your brother Aaron with you. I will speak through you both. Go, and lead my people. *(Turns US.)*

4: So they went.

5: And they did.

(All move to form staggered line SL of GOD. *2 moves DSR.)*

1: Now many years later

3: The Lord spoke to Jonah.

1: He said:

GOD: *(turning DS)* I have a task for you.

5: And Jonah said:

2/JONAH: Whoops, I'm off. *(Walks behind* GOD, *who turns US. 4, 5 form a 'ship' with bodies MSC,* JONAH *appears in it.)*

1: *(SL)* And ran away to sea.

2/JONAH: *(singing)* Life on the ocean wave,

3: But God made the wind blow *(1, 3 blow, 'ship' rocks)*, and the sailors said: *(1 and 3 join 'ship'.)*

SAILORS 1, 3: Help! Help!

3: And Jonah said:

2/JONAH: It's all my fault. Throw me overboard.

1: So they did. *(*SAILORS *throw Jonah overboard by pushing him through 'ship'.)* And the sea calmed. *(3, 4, 5 adopt 'whale' shape.)*

1: *(SR)* And the whale said:

WHALE 3, 4, 5: *(as they engulf* JONAH*)* Gulp! *(Appropriate burping noise.)*

1: But, being fairly fussy about its food:

WHALE: Huh! *(sick noise.)*

1: Brought up Jonah to dry land. *(*JONAH *rolls forward,*

'whale' unforms 1, 3 *SL*—4, 5 *SR.)*

5: And Jonah said:

2/JONAH: *(DSC)* The Lord has saved me. Deliverance belongs to him.

4: And the Lord said:

GOD: *(turning)* Now will you go to Nineveh?

3: And Jonah said:

2/JONAH: Yes.

1, 3, 4, 5: Hurray! *(*1, 3 *stagger from* GOD*;* 2, 4 *stagger SR from* GOD. 5 *USC, back to audience, just in front of* GOD.*)*

3: Now, many years later,

4: The Father turned *(*GOD *turns)* to his Son and said:

GOD: I have a task for you.

4: And the Son said:

5/JESUS: *(turning DS)* Here I am, send me.

3: And the Father said:

GOD: It will mean pain, hatred, derision, unbelief, betrayal, and death.

2: And the Son said:

5/JESUS: Let your will be done.

1: And the Father said:

GOD: It is the only way they can meet me, turn to me and love me. I give you my power and authority.

4: And weeping, he sent his Son:

GOD: Go now, and save my people.

3: And the Son went and obeyed.

5/JESUS: *(moves DSC)* Nothing I do or say is on my own authority, but on the authority of him who sent me.

As they speak 4, 2 *circle round to the left*—1, 5 *to right. Both towards DSC. As they reach Jesus, he steps back and shrinks to the floor, hidden by* 1, 2, 3, 4.*)*

1: And the Son went,

2: And was hated,

3: Was betrayed,

4: Was beaten. *(They stop, face audience.)*

1, 2, 3, 4: And died. *(Pause.)*

2: And, defeating death *(*5/JESUS *pushes* 1, 2, 3, 4 *apart, they stand on original sides, DS.)*

3: He rose again,

4: And echoing his Father's words,
1: He said,
5/JESUS: *(to people and audience)* Go into the world and tell them about me. *(Goes SR.)*
3: Many years later
4: The Lord still speaks.
GOD: I have a task for you.
1, 2, 3, 4, 5: Who us? *(to audience)* For us. *(Pause.)*
GOD: *(to audience)* And for you.
1, 2, 3, 4, 5: *(to audience)* For you.

You Can Have Me on Sunday, Lord

A sketch about following Jesus and the consequent effects on our lives, our priorities and our time. For both Christians and non-Christians.

CHARACTERS: JESUS
BUSINESSMAN

SCENE: *An office. The* BUSINESSMAN *is working intently at his desk, SC three-quarters to audience. Enter* JESUS *SL, moving towards the desk. He waits, but the* BUSINESSMAN *continues working.*

JESUS: Hello.
MAN *(not looking up)*: Do you have an appointment?
JESUS: You asked me to come, remember?
MAN: Can't say I do, no. What was the name?
JESUS: Jesus Christ, Son of God.
MAN: Well, if you'd like to leave your name with my secretary—*(looks up, startled)*. I'm sorry, what did you say?
JESUS: Jesus Christ, Son of God.
MAN: And I—asked you to come?
JESUS: You invited me into your life, yes.

MAN: Well, er, yes, you're, er, very welcome. *(Pause. Looks round, embarrassed.)* Er, when exactly was this?

JESUS: Last Sunday, at church.

MAN: Oh yes, I never miss a service.

JESUS: Quite, and when the minister called on everyone to commit their lives to me, you did so gladly.

MAN: Of course, only too delighted to.

JESUS: Good. Come on then, follow me.

MAN: Pardon?

JESUS: You said you'd follow.

MAN: Er, yes, I mean, er, well, er, what I actually meant was... when I said, er, but that was then.

JESUS: Have you changed your mind?

MAN: Er, no, no. Of course not. What do you mean?

JESUS: To trust me, with all you have—even your life.

MAN: My life?

JESUS: Yes. I want you to live my life, full life. I have a plan for you—and that plan is better than anything you could wish for yourself. Trust me—follow me.

MAN: Er, yes, of course. Delighted to. Now, the only problem is, when? *(Flicks through his diary.)* Now let's see. Monday is bridge night, Tuesday, deacons' meeting, Wednesday, Board meeting.

JESUS: Now.

MAN: I beg your pardon?

JESUS: Now.

MAN: Now? Oh, but that's impossible. After all, there are arrangements to, er, arrange. Things to be done.

JESUS: Follow me now. I will give you rest from all the things that need to be done. I'll help you do them in my time, not yours. But first you must follow.

MAN: Yes, er...

JESUS: Choose my way instead of yours. If you cherish your own life instead of the life I can give you, you'll lose that life.

Silence.

I'm not going to force you. I'm offering you new life.

MAN: I see. Well, you've given me something to think about.

When I called you on Sunday, I wasn't quite ready for—this.

JESUS: You did not call me. I have called you.

MAN: That's as maybe, but I'm not sure I'm ready to be called. I'll do my best of course. I'll stick with this church-going business.

JESUS: I want obedience and commitment, not sacrifice. Not everyone who says to me, 'Lord, Lord' will enter the Kingdom of heaven. I called you, but you did not follow. The day may come when I have to say to you, 'I never knew you.' *(Turns to leave. Turns back.)* I said I would never force you. *(Exits SL.)*

MAN: But—I say—will I see you on Sunday?

The Ticket Office

A sketch about 'getting into' heaven.

CHARACTERS: THE TICKET COLLECTOR
MAN
TWO WOMEN

SCENE: *An empty stage. The* TICKET COLLECTOR *stands near the centre. A* WOMAN *approaches.*

TICKET COLLECTOR: Tickets please. *(*WOMAN *gives the* COLLECTOR *her ticket to be inspected.)* Thank you, madam. Go straight through.

(Enter MAN *looking around him in wonder. Doesn't notice the* TICKET COLLECTOR *and bumps into him.)*

MAN: I say, I'm terribly sorry. Is this really heaven?

T.C.: No, sir, not quite. This is the Ticket Office.

MAN: I didn't know you had to have a ticket to get in. I

thought anybody could go in.

T.C.: Oh no, sir.

MAN: I see. Oh well, it makes sense—after all, we don't want just anybody do we? I'll have an off-peak single then. I don't think I'll be needing a return.

T.C.: Er, no, sir, you can't buy them here. You have to hand them into me, and if everything is in order, I let you through.

MAN: *(slightly deflated)* Well, where can I get one then?

T.C.: All tickets have to be acquired on earth, sir.

MAN: I say, that's a bit awkward. I can't really go back, can I?

T.C.: No, sir.

MAN: *(realizing)* Wait a minute. I've just remembered. I think I have one somewhere.

T.C.: Jolly good, sir. *(*MAN *digs into pockets and pulls out a ticket.)*

MAN: Yes, here it is.

T.C.: *(reading)* 'This is to certify that the bearer of this ticket has always led a good life. *(*MAN *smiles piously)* was faithful to his wife...

MAN: Well, most of the time...

T.C.: Loved his kids, gave to charities, was always kind and courteous...'

MAN: Well, to most people anyway. I mean, the neighbours get on my wick a bit at times, but one just has to get on the best one can with such pompous, ill mannered...

T.C.: Er, quite, sir, quite. I'm afraid this ticket isn't valid.

MAN: Isn't valid. But it must be. It's got all the right information, hasn't it?

T.C.: I'm afraid it expired when you did. Perhaps you have another one somewhere?

MAN: *(delving into pockets)* Yes, let's see. *(Finds one.)* Ah, here we are.

T.C.: *(taking second ticket)* 'This is to certify that the bearer is of sound mind and body. He can run a mile in just under five minutes, has swum the channel.'

MAN: And back again.

T.C.: 'And was a boxing champion at school. He has twelve

'O' levels, five 'A' levels and a B.A. in Business Studies. He is, in short, pretty clever.'

MAN: I think that sums me up rather well.

T.C.: 'And his modesty is second to none.'

MAN: True, true.

T.C.: That's as maybe sir, but this just won't do.

MAN: Why not?

T.C.: It's not valid for entry, sir.

MAN: Well, I don't think I've got another one.

T.C.: Then I'm afraid I can't let you in.

MAN: Look, you must have some tickets around here somewhere. I'll buy one from you now. I'll pay as much as you want.

T.C.: *(indignantly)* I've told you, I don't sell tickets—anyway, they're given away.

MAN: *(incredulously)* Given away? Then how come I didn't get one?

T.C.: Perhaps you never asked for one, sir.

(WOMAN enters. Hands ticket to Ticket Collector.)

T.C.: Thank you, madam. Go straight in.

MAN: She got in all right. It's sex discrimination, that's what it is.

T.C.: She gave me the right ticket, sir. That's all.

MAN: *(taking ticket)* Here, let me see. 'This is to certify that the bearer has accepted Jesus Christ as her Saviour and Lord; that she acknowledges that his blood was shed on the cross as an act of love for her, forgiving her for everything she has done wrong, paying for the gift of eternal life; and that since she accepted the gift she has lived her life in obedience to Christ.'

T.C.: Perhaps you have a ticket like that somewhere, sir?

MAN: *(dejected)* No, I don't believe I have.

T.C.: Then I'm sorry, sir.

MAN: Look, couldn't you let me through a side entrance? I mean I'd make it worth your while.

T.C.: Sorry, sir. There is only one entrance. Perhaps you'd better try downstairs.

(The MAN turns away. Both freeze.)

If You're Too Busy to Pray . . .

A sketch for Christians, dealing with the priorities in our lives. (Stresses are shown with a ´ to emphasize scansion.)

CHARACTERS: A, B and C—three people who have overslept
NARRATOR
JESUS
A FEW FOLLOWERS

SCENE: *An untidy room.* A *lies asleep in bed. An alarm clock rings.* A *stretches and after a while looks at the clock. On seeing the time he shrieks and leaps out of bed. To the sound of fast music (optional—e.g. chase music from silent movies, or 'Flight of the Bumble Bee', etc.) he starts rushing around, putting on clothes, etc.* B *enters at exactly the same pace, gathering up things and putting them into a bag.* C *enters, frantically eating breakfast. After a short period of hectic activity, the three start rushing off, all still only half ready. As they go SR, the* NARRATOR *blows a whistle. They stop and turn back MSC.*

NARRATOR: Haven't you forgotten something?
(The three look at each other blankly, and then suddenly realize what they've forgotten. They get in line, kneel down and adopt a prayer-like pose.)

A B & C: *(in unison)* Hélp us Lórd this dáy we práy,
But we ásk please dón't get iń the wáy.
Gránt us thát we míght get thŕough
Aĺl the thíngs we háve to d́o.
We'd gíve more t́ime but ẃe've not ǵot it,
I pŕayed last Túesday, díd you sṕot it?
We ćan't give ýou our fúll atteńtion,

But there áre some things we óught to mention:
With so much work left ón our hands
We'd be grateful íf you'd bless our plans;
And ás we rush through éach packed hour,
Please be sure you don't spoil óur—
Rhythm.

(A, B & C freeze as JESUS *enters with small crowd around him.)*

NARRATOR: Jesus continued on his whirlwind tour. *(One of his entourage produces a map to show him the next stop on the route.)* Galilee, Capernaum, next stop, Jerusalem. He moved impatiently away from the crowd as a woman tried to touch him. He had no time to heal the sick or comfort the afflicted. Soon they'd be asking him to take children on his knee. Whatever next? Did they expect him to give his whole life? He had no time. He had far more important things to do....

*(*JESUS *turns his back on the pleading crowd and freezes. As he does so,* A, B & C *come to life again.)*

A B & C: *(in unison)* Úse our lives so Lord, we pray,
But don't disrúpt our well-planned day.
Help us Lord this day we pray,
But we ásk please don't get ín the way.
Help us Lord this day we pray,
Help us Lord this day... *(pause)*
Help us Lord... *(pause)*
Help.

(During the last sequence of 'Help us, Lord' their voices slowly fade, fading away completely, on the final cry, 'Help'.)

Seventy Times Seven

A sketch about forgiveness, principally for Christians.

CHARACTERS: SIR, an executive
ROBERTS, an underling

SCENE: SIR'S *office.* SIR *is sitting at a desk on which there is a telephone. The desk is angled towards the audience. There is a knock OSR.*

SIR: Enter *(Enter* ROBERTS *SR.)* Ah, there you are. Now look here, Roberts. I'm extremely angry about the mess you've made of these figures. *(*ROBERTS *stands, quivering.)* I mean, just look at this. They're all in the wrong columns, and none of them tally, and what on earth is this brown patch all over the debit column?

ROBERTS *(Peering at the figures)*: A c-coffee stain, s-sir.

SIR: A coffee stain! *(*ROBERTS *cringes.)* What are our auditors going to think if all our books are covered in coffee!

ROBERTS: I'm s-sorry s-sir. It was an accident, sir. Please forgive me, sir. It won't happen again. I'm really very...

SIR: Yes, all right, don't go on. I'll let you off this time. *(Looks through file.)* Now, let me see, ah, here we are, Roberts, *(writing)* four hundred and eighty-nine. Now, what's this I hear about our new shockproof, *break*proof, indestructible guaranteed-lifetime computer?

ROBERTS: What about it sir?

SIR: You broke it, Roberts.

ROBERTS *(on his knees)*: Oh yes sir, I'm terribly sorry, please forgive me, sir. It was all my fault. You see it was an accident.

SIR: I thought you said it was all your fault.

ROBERTS: Yes, er, I mean it was all my fault the accident happened. My foot slipped. I'm sorry, sir.

SIR *(grudgingly)*: Well, all right, but see that it doesn't happen again. *(Writing in the book.)* Four hundred and ninety.

ROBERTS: Thank you, sir. *(Turns. Starts to creep slowly off.)*

SIR: Just a moment, Roberts. *(*ROBERTS *freezes, face to audience, cringing anticipating something awful.)* There's just the little matter of my car.

ROBERTS: Ah.

SIR: Quite.

ROBERTS: *(turning)* I will pay for repairs to the paintwork, sir.

SIR: And the dented door?

ROBERTS: And the dented door, sir.

SIR: And the wing mirror?

ROBERTS: Yes, sir.

SIR: And the windscreen, the headlights, the bonnet, and the roof?

ROBERTS: Y-yes, sir.

SIR: Really, Roberts this is not good enough. I'm afraid this is unforgivable.

ROBERTS: But, sir,

SIR: No, I'm sorry. In any case *(looks at book, grins)* you've had your quota!

ROBERTS: Sir?

SIR: Company rules clearly state, 'Four hundred and ninety apologies to be accepted.' To forgive you a four hundred and ninety-first time would clearly contravene the company charter.

ROBERTS: But, sir, it doesn't say four hundred and ninety, it says seventy times seven.

SIR: Which equals four hundred and ninety. No wonder you're a useless accountant if you can't even work that out.

ROBERTS: But it was only a guide set down by management to indicate that errors should always be forgiven, sir.

SIR: I've got better things to do than to sit around forgiving your incompetent blunders all day. You're finished, do you understand?

ROBERTS: But, sir, please forgive me. Just give me one more chance. Please!

SIR: Stop grovelling, you snivelling little worm. Go on, get out!

ROBERTS: But, sir.

SIR: Out! *(Exit* ROBERTS, *dismally SL.)* Insolent buffoon. *(Picks up phone.)* Hello, Beatrice, can you put me through to the boss, please? *(Taps on table, muttering to himself while waiting to be connected)*...Ah, hallo, sir, I thought I ought to let you know. There's been a bit of a scene here. I'm afraid I've had to let Roberts go...Why? Well, he's been making such terrible blunders, and then expects me to forgive him. I mean, what a nerve.... What do you mean I should have done?... Yes, sir, I do know what you said about forgiveness, and believe me I've followed it to the letter.... No, really. Seventy times seven you said.... What was that... By that you mean infinity? *(Chuckling.)* Oh, come now, you can't be serious? You don't really want me to forgive scum like Roberts indefinitely, I mean that's just too much.... Yes sir, I know you've often had cause to forgive me, but not as many as four hundred and ninety.... *(Laughs, and then mouth drops in shock.)* Er, how many times did you say?... Oh, come now, you're pulling my.... You're not? Well, I'm really sorry, sir, I had no idea.... What's that?... You can't accept my apology? Oh, come now, if you've already accepted so many, what difference does one more make?... You can't forgive me until I've forgiven Roberts? Don't you think that's a little unreasonable?... No, I know you're not obliged to forgive me, but I... but... but.... Oh, all right then I'll forgive the greasy little swine... what do you mean that's not good enough? I'm forgiving the creep aren't I? *(Horrified.)* Graciously? Why should I be gracious to that horrible little... Because you're always gracious to me. But you don't have to put up with his blundering and idiotic.... What do you mean, you have to put up with my self-righteous attitude? *(Shouting.)* I am not self-righteous! *(Normal.)* Besides, I can't forgive him now, I mean, I have my pride to think of.... What's that... You don't like pride... well, I guess you win... Yes, sir... No, sir.... Yes, graciously, sir.... I'm sorry, sir.... Right away, sir. Goodbye, sir....

(Pause to collect himself.) Beatrice, send Roberts in again will you?

Can't Do That

A sketch about how Jesus put individuals above traditions and about how his breach of traditions eventually became unacceptable to the upholders of them. A clapping rhythm to a steady 4/4 time is heard throughout the sketch, except where indicated, and the timing of each line is very important. The clapping can either be done by the crowd as they go about their business, or as a sound effect by someone off stage.

CHARACTERS: CROWD, *not too large, but with at least four. The four speaking parts and* PILATE *can be drawn from the crowd, but do not all need to be different.*

SCENE: *A busy street in Jerusalem. The crowd is going about its daily business, stopping only to hear the latest gossip about a strange man from Nazareth. Each speaker moves among the crowd in time to the rhythm, and spreads the latest news, milling. 1st moves to SC, crowd gather in open horseshoe. Clicking rhythm begins. The action should be 'natural'. 'Beats' indicate clicks to keep rhythm. Lines should be syncopated. On 'clap' all clap together.*

(4 beats)

1ST: Have you h̀eard the wòrd?

(2 beats)

CROWD: What wòrd?

1ST: *(beat)* The wòrd about the m̀an from Ṇàzareth̀.

CROWD: What màn? *(beat)*

1ST: The màn who healed the màn with the wìthered hànd.

CROWD: Hè did t̀hat? *(beat)* But that's gòod.

1ST: *(beat)* No wàit. *(click)*

CROWD: There's m̀ore? *(clap.) (Clicking ceases.)*

1ST: *(beckoning them round, confidentially)* He did it on the Sabbath.

2ND: *(with shocked gasps)* But he can't do that!
CROWD: Can't do that.
1ST: He just *did. (Rhythm begins again. Crowd move on.* 2ND *emerges on 'did'.)*
2ND: *(3 beats)* Have you hèard the wòrd?
CROWD: *(2 beats)* What wòrd?
2ND: *(beat)* The wòrd about the màn from Nàzarèth.
CROWD: That màn agaìn! *(2 beats)*
2ND: They tèll me he spòke to a wòman. *(beat)*
CROWD: A ràbbi who spòke to a wòman? *(beat)*
2ND: A Samàritan wòman. *(Clap.) (Rhythm ceases)*... with a very dubious background. *(breath intake)*
3RD: *(obviously shocked)* But he can't do that.
CROWD: Can't do that!
2ND: He just *did. (3 beats)*

(The CROWD *move on. The rhythm begins again on 'did'.* 3RD *emerges.)*

(4 beats)

3RD: Have you heàrd the wòrd?

(2 beats)

CROWD: What wòrd?
3RD: *(beat)* The wòrd about the màn from Nàzarèth.
CROWD: What nòw? *(beat)*
3RD: They sày that hè's been sèen aròund with sìnners. *(beat)*
CROWD: With sìnners? *(beat)*
3RD: *(lowering voice)* He dìnes with thèm.
CROWD: Where wìll this ènd?
3RD: He toùches thèm.
CROWD: *(pulling faces of disgust)* This càn't go òn.
3RD: Forgìving thèm! *(Clap! Rhythm stops.)*
4TH: But he can't do that! *(Rhythm stops.)*
CROWD: Càn't do thàt!
3RD: But he does. *(3 beats)*

(Rhythm starts again on 'does'. CROWD *start moving again.* 4TH *emerges.)*

4TH: Have you hèard the wòrd?
CROWD: Oh nòt agaìn!
4TH: They sày that he's crìticized the Phariseès.

CROWD: He càn't do thàt!
4TH: Told thèm they're wròng!
CROWD: He càn't do thàt!
4TH: Càlled them hỳpocrites!
CROWD: He càn't do thàt!
4TH: And whìtewashed tòmbs! *(Clap! (Rhythm stops.))*
PHARISEE: *(as rest of crowd gasp)* He definitely can't do that.

(The CROWD *splits into two,* CROWD A *questioning SL,* CROWD B, *responding SR. Rhythm starts again.)*
(8 beats starting on the word 'that'.)

CROWD A: Hèaling on the Sàbbath?
CROWD B: He càn't do thàt.
CROWD A: Tàlks with wòmen?
CROWD B: It's gòt to stòp.
CROWD A: Forgìving like a gòd.
CROWD B: Put an ènd to thàt.
CROWD A: Upsètting our lìves.
CROWD B: Put an ènd to hìm! *(2 beats)*
PILATE: *(Emerging from crowd DSR)* You can hàve the last wòrd.
CROWD: *(massing SL)* We wànt him dèad.
PILATE: That's your fìnal wòrd?
CROWD: Free Baràbbas insteàd. *(Clicking gets louder.)*
PILATE: I wash my hànds of this affàir.
CROWD: Crùcify! Crùcify!
PILATE: Have him kìlled if you dàre. *(Moves DSR.)*
CROWD: Fìnish it! Fìnish it! *(Clap)*

There is silence as the CROWD *turn with their backs to the audience. The sound of the banging of nails is heard three times DSR. Then silence for a moment before the* CROWD *turn and resume their business except* PILATE *who remains DSR, facing US some people showing relief, others strangely subdued, continually looking back at what they've just done. As they get back into the rhythm of their lives again,* 1ST *emerges once more to begin clicking rhythm.*
(4 beats)

1ST: Have you heàrd the wòrd?
CROWD: *(2 beats)* What wòrd?
1ST: *(beat)* The wòrd about the màn from Nàzarèth.

CROWD: But he's deàd. *(beat).*
1ST: No he aìn't. *(beat).*
CROWD: *(shocked)* He aìn't? *(beat)*
1ST: They sày all they fòund was an eṁpty gràve.
CROWD: An èmpty gravè? *(2 beats)*
1ST: They sày he's been seèn.
CROWD: *(2 beats)* Been sèen? *(beat)* But hoẁ? *(Clap. Rhythm stops.)* But how?
1ST: They tell me he's risen from the dead.

*(Pause—*CROWD *look at one another, shocked.)*

PILATE: *(turning)* But he can't do that!

(All freeze.)

Supersaviour

A sketch about what would probably happen if man attempted to put together his own 'Supersaviour' using all the ingredients commonly seen as important.

CHARACTERS: DR KLAUS VON SCHWINKELMEYER, *yet another mad German scientist.*
THE INGREDIENTS: *2 politicians, a peace-keeper, 2 soldiers, a doctor, a scientist, a psychoanalyst, an athlete, a literary figure, a musician, all of which can be men or women.*
2 V.I.P.*'s*
SUPERSAVIOUR

SCENE: *The mad doctor's laboratory. On stage is a large box or screen. As can be seen, a lot of people are needed for this sketch, so the screen could be arranged to allow for some doubling up.*

KLAUS *(entering, muttering to himself)*: Oh boy, zey've really gone and done it zis time. Nincompoops! How am I supposed to... *(sees audience and turns to address them).* Oh, gut evenink. Klaus von Schwinkelmeyer, zee vurld's number vun scientist at your service. I heff zis teency weency little problem vich hess almost even ze great Schwinkelmeyer beaten. Almost, but not qvite. You see ze powers zat be heff decided in zeyre great visdom zat ze vurld, being as it iss in ein grossen mess, ist in need of sumvun who can save it. Und since nun of zee applicants were gut enough, ze brilliant me hess to make vun. Seemple, huh? Zis man must have all ze qualities zat you vould expect ein Saviour to heff. He must be ecceptable to everyvun, all races, creeds and shades of political opinion. As you can see, nussing too complicated. Neffer mind. Ze great Schwinkelmeyer vill not be beaten. I shall look in my menuel. *(Dusts off large book and flicks through pages.)* Ah, here ve are. Saviour, ingredients for. Hmm. Zey don't need ein scientist but ein master chef. First vee need zwei politician, ein left vun. *(Enter* LEFT POLITICIAN.*)*

L.P.: Power to the people! All property is theft! Nationalize all wealth!

KLAUS: Yes, sank you very much. Into ze box pleese. Und also ein right vun. *(Enter* RIGHT POLITICIAN.*)*

R.P.: We must fight the socialist menace. We must keep our pride in the very institutions that have made our country great.

KLAUS: Yes, verry gut. In ze box please. *(*R.P. *enters the box.)* Ve also need ein renowned peacekeeper to sort out ze squabbles.

(Enter PEACEKEEPER, *backing away from two soldiers with guns.)*

PEACEKEEPER: Er now, listen, chaps. Let's talk this over. I mean, now, don't let's do anything hasty, huh? I mean, come on fellas, be reasonable. *(The* SOLDIERS *push him into the box.)*

KLAUS: Und ein military brain. *(*SOLDIERS *point their guns at him.)* Er, zwei military brains. *(*SOLDIERS *enter box.)* Well, zwei military, anyway. *(A shot is fired)* I didn't mean it, fellas, really. Und ve need ein doctor to deal vith all ze vurld's medical problems. *(Looks at box.)* Especially ze vuns caused by these crazy gun happy... *(another shot is* *fired)*...okay, I'm sorry, I'm sorry. *(Enter* DOCTOR.*)*

DOCTOR: Yes, what seems to be the trouble? Breathe in, nothing to worry about. Keep taking the tablets. *(Reaches Klaus.)* Yes, what seems to be the trouble? Breathe in. *(Plunges stethoscope into Klaus' chest.)*

KLAUS: Get off. *(Pushes him into the box.)*

DOCTOR: Keep taking the tablets.

KLAUS: Und ein psychoanalyst to deal viz all ze emotional problems of zee vurld. *(Enter* PSYCHOANALYST.*)*

PSYCHO: Now just lie back and relax, and tell me about your childhood. What do you mean you had a wonderful childhood? You should be so lucky. I had a terrible childhood. We were so poor my brother was made in Hong Kong.

KLAUS *(pushing him into the box)*: There, there. Perhaps you should see a— vell, no, on second thoughts, perhaps you'd better not. Now zen, vat's next? Ah yes, someone to cater for people's spiritual needs. Oh, but zere are so many. Vich vun? Vich vun? O vell, ve'll skip zat vun, it probably isn't very important. No one vill notice. Und finally, vee need a little culture, a little azleticism. Can ve have ze vurld's leading musician, ze leading literary figure, ze best azlete, und ze vurld's best scientist, no, vait a minute, zat's me. Ze vurld's second most eminent scientist please.

(Enter MUSICIAN, *playing instrument,* ATHLETE *saying, 'I am de greatest' and miming some sport,* LITERARY FIGURE *reciting Shakespeare, and* SCIENTIST *with test tube etc.)*

(All move quickly into the box. SCIENTIST *turns to Klaus.)*

SCIENTIST: I still say I was the best. *(Enters box haughtily.)*

KLAUS: At last, that is all. Yes, vell, at last I zink ve're ready. Ve must now stir ze ingredients togezer. *(Stands on chair, and stirs with a large spoon.)* adding in ein peench of colouring, ein little vite ein little black, yellow, brown— oh, and I mustn't forget ze languages *(throws in some phrase books)* French, Italian, Swahili, Cantonese. Und now ve vill svitch on ze machine.

(Enter two V.I.P*'s)*

1ST: Ah, Dr Winkelmeyer.

KLAUS: Schwinkelmeyer.

2ND: Quite. How are the experiments to find Supersaviour going?

KLAUS: Gentlemen, stand back and prepare to be amazed.

(The box begins to shake, rocked by those inside it. Eventually a man leaps out. His face is striped different colours, and he is wearing a Superman type tee-shirt.)

KLAUS: Gentlemen, is it not amazing?

1ST *(uncertain)*: Yes. It certainly is, er, er, different.

2ND: Are you Supersaviour, the person who will save mankind?

SUPERSAVIOUR: What seems to be the trouble?

1ST *(Taken aback)*: Well, the whole world's in chaos, a state of open rebellion against all authority.

SUPERSAVIOUR: Long live the revolution. Nationalize all wealth.

2ND: Er, well, that's not quite what we intended. We hoped you could help.

SUPERSAVIOUR: Sure, sure. Now lie back and relax and tell me about your childhood.

1ST: What's that got to do with it?

SUPERSAVIOUR: I don't know, I had a terrible childhood. My mother...

2ND: Look, can you help us or not?

SUPERSAVIOUR: Urglewimblyopplydoopoopadoopdewhapshowadywaddyneeersplat *(or some such incomprehensible phrase)*.

1ST: Well, what does that mean?

SUPERSAVIOUR: It's Swahili for, 'There is a skunk in my woodpile.' Can I have my violin please?

2ND: The man is a complete idiot. How can we put our trust in him?

SUPERSAVIOUR: That is the question.

KLAUS: Gentlemen, he is only in his early stages of development. I can rebuild him. I have ze technology.

1ST: No, I'm sorry, this isn't going to work. *(They turn away.)*

KLAUS: But, gentlemen.

SUPERSAVIOUR: Keep taking the pills.

KLAUS: Oh, shut up. *(Kicks Supersaviour.)*

SUPERSAVIOUR *(looking angry)*: I am de greatest. *(Punches Klaus on the nose. They freeze as conversation between* V.I.P*'s continues. Stage slap.)*

2ND: But we do need someone.

1ST: We'll just have to look through the files again.

2ND: What about that first chap?

1ST: The Jew? Would anyone listen to him?

2ND: Well, he's the only one who spoke with any sort of authority.

1ST: And he did heal people.

2ND: He did have some funny ideas, though.

1ST: Quite. Like rising from the dead.

2ND: And actually loving our enemies.

1ST: That wouldn't go down well, I can tell you.

2ND: And saying he was the Son of God.

1ST: Who?

2ND: Strange, though. Willing to die for his cause.

1ST: And yet he never used violent methods himself.

2ND: He seemed pretty sure he was the only answer for the world, didn't he?

1ST: Yes, but we couldn't possibly have chosen him. He'd never have fitted in with our way of doing things.

2ND: Didn't seem as if he was going to try.

1ST: And after all, he was only a carpenter.

(They shake their heads and exit. As they go the words, 'Well why don't we form a committee' *are heard.)*

Darkness and Light

A sketch contrasting two opposite worlds. It requires some lighting effects, preferably a follow spot.

CHARACTERS: JESUS
A
B
PEOPLE IN DARKNESS, *among whom four voices are heard during the sketch*

SCENE: *A darkened stage. A group of people can just be seen, stumbling around blindly. Theirs is a harsh, cruel world. They bump into one another, push each other around, sometimes violently and abuse one another. Cries of 'Out of the way', 'Look where you're going', 'Can't see', 'Tread on me again and I'll kill you' are heard ad lib, as a sense of confusion is conveyed. Eventually a desperate voice is heard.*

VOICE 1: Will somebody please give us some light?

(Very suddenly, a spotlight is switched on, and JESUS, *dressed in white, stands at the centre of that light. Immediately, shocked by the bright contrast, all but one of the crowd shield their eyes and turn away.)*

VOICES: Aahh. Too bright, man. Turn it down.

(The lone figure, A, *approaches the light and steps into it.)*

A *(staring around, blinking)*: Hey, this is great. I can actually see where I'm going.

VOICE 1: Don't be a fool. Come back out here where it's safe.

A: No, it feels much safer here. I can see. The darkness and confusion have gone.

JESUS: I am the light. Darkness has no place here.

VOICE 2: Come back over here, where your friends are.

VOICE 3: Yeah, don't be an idiot. People will see you.

*(*A *pauses, uncertainly, and then runs towards the edge of the light, to rejoin the others. He stops, confused.)*

A: Wait a minute, it's getting darker.

JESUS: Light cannot have fellowship with darkness. If you love the light, walk in it.

*(*A *moves back to* JESUS. *The* PEOPLE *begin stumbling around again.)*

A *(rather proudly)*: Look at them, the fools. They haven't found what I've found. Somebody ought to tell them. My way is best. *(As he has been speaking this line he has been moving further and further from the centre of the light.)*

JESUS: It isn't your way. You can do nothing for them, except through me. If you don't love, how can you provide them with any light.

A *(very superior)*: But I'm all right. I've seen the light. *(He rushes back into the darkness and tries to attract his friends.)* Listen. You've got to listen to me. I've seen the light. I've found somewhere much better than this.

(The voices mock him.)

VOICE 1: Who said that?

VOICE 2: I see no light.

VOICE 3: You're no different from us. What have you got to show for it?

VOICE 4: Stay here with us. *(Tempting.)* You can have more fun in the dark.

*(*A *appears uncertain. They take hold of him. He turns away from them and reaches back out to the light, where* JESUS *reaches out and pulls him in.)*

A *(Exhausted)*: What went wrong?

JESUS: You were doing it your way, not mine. You became proud and plunged yourself straight back into darkness. If you tell people there is light, and have none to show them, how are they going to believe? Come on, let's try again. Only this time, stick with me.

*(*JESUS *walks towards the* PEOPLE. A *stays close to him. As they move, the light moves with them. The* PEOPLE *turn away.)*

VOICE 1: No. Stop him. It's too bright.

VOICE 2: He'll see what we're doing.

VOICE 3: He'll expose us.

(As the light begins to fall upon them, the PEOPLE *move away again out of it. One solitary figure turns and stares at the light, and at* A. B *walks towards the light and hovers on the edge.* A *steps towards her.)*

B: But you're different. You've changed. *(Looks from* A *to* JESUS.*)* You begin to look like light itself.

A: Come into the light. It's better here. All the confusion seems to have disappeared.

B: But—I don't know. I mean, to leave behind...

A: All you have to leave behind is a world of darkness and confusion. Light and darkness can't exist together. You must choose one or the other.

*(*B *hovers for a moment, and then makes a move towards* A.*)*

VOICE 1 (*suddenly turning*): Oh, I can't take any more of this. Will somebody please turn the light off.

VOICES: Turn it off, turn it off.

A: But the light was given for you to see. You asked for it.

VOICES: Turn it off, turn it off.

VOICE 1: That was before. It's too powerful.

VOICES: Turn it off. Turn it off.

(The PEOPLE *rush at Jesus.* A & B *turn away. As the* PEOPLE *grab hold of Jesus, the light goes out. There is darkness once more.)*

VOICE 1: That's better.

VOICE 2: I'm not so sure, now.

(Light falls on A & B. *A voice shouts at* A.*)*

VOICE 3: Hey, weren't you one of those who walked in the light?

A: Who, me? No, no. *(Looks at* B, *grief-stricken.)* Oh, what have I said?

B: Look!

(The stage is fully lit. JESUS *stands at the centre. Most of the* PEOPLE *fall to their knees.* 1 *and* 3 *back off.)*

VOICES 1 & 3: No, it can't be. I can't stand it. Must find somewhere to hide. *(They exit hurriedly off either side of the stage.)*

(All freeze as B *speaks.)*

B: The light shines in the darkness, but the darkness has not understood it. The true light that gives light to every man has come into the world.

Good News

A sketch about reactions to Christ's rising from the dead.

CHARACTERS: PASSERS-BY *in a busy street in Jerusalem. From them several pairs emerge:* TWO RICH AND POWERFUL FIGURES, A SCRIBE AND A PHARISEE, PILATE AND CAIAPHAS, PETER AND MARY. *Others in the street make passing comments:* THOMAS, NICODEMUS, THE CENTURION, *etc*
TWO DARK FIGURES *are positioned to one side of the stage*
THE NEWS SELLER
Table for basic props USL.

SCENE: *A bustling street in Jerusalem. As the* NEWS-SELLER *shouts out USR on box 1-5 go about their business. Carefully staged street scene. During the conversations the characters not involved remain still.*

NEWS SELLER: *(USR on box)* Read all about it. Good News. Read all about it.

PASSERS-BY: Good news? What does he mean? Nothing good ever happens. What good news?

NEWS SELLER: Jesus of Nazareth Lives. Eye Witness Account. Read all about it.

PASSERS-BY: Alive? But he can't be. We saw him die.

(3 and 4 go USR, clip on ties/hats, return to face audience.)

NEWS SELLER: Read all about it! Good News! Jesus Lives! Questions raised in high society. *(Still, watches action.)*

(3 and 4 become RICH *and* POWERFUL *and come forward anxiously.)*

RICH: Did you hear that?

POWERFUL: Good news, he said.

RICH: Don't like the sound of it.

POWERFUL: Could have implications.

RICH: Might affect our position.

POWERFUL: Our wealth and power.

RICH: Our peace of mind.

POWERFUL: If it's true.

RICH: Can't be true. If he was dead on Friday...

POWERFUL: ...He can't be alive today.

RICH: Impossible. Just couldn't happen.

POWERFUL: Just rumours. Nothing will come of them.

RICH: Thank goodness for that.

BOTH: Well, you've really eased my mind...and yet...

NEWS SELLER: Read all about it. Tomb Found Empty. Jesus Alive.

(5 and 6 become TWO CENTURIONS *and walk past the news seller. Their attention is caught by his cries.)*

1ST CENTURION: Alive? How can he be? You saw him die, didn't you.

2ND CENTURION: Oh, he was dead all right. But believe me, after what I witnessed on that day anything is possible.

1ST CENTURION: Don't start that 'Son of God' talk again or you won't stay a centurion for long, I can tell you. *(They continue on their way, merge once more into the other passers-by.)*

(1 and 2 make their way USL to collect props.)

NEWS SELLER: Read all about it. Jesus Alive. Good News. Religious Leaders Puzzled.

(1 and 2 are now SCRIBE *and* PHARISEE, *and come forward.)*

SCRIBE: What's this I hear?

PHARISEE: Risen from the dead?

SCRIBE: Impossible.

PHARISEE: But if it's true...

SCRIBE: It'd muck up our religion, that's for sure.

PHARISEE: People might start to listen to him.
SCRIBE: Instead of us.
PHARISEE: Still...
SCRIBE: Probably nothing in it.
PHARISEE: After all, there's nothing in Scripture to support it.
SCRIBE: There is.
PHARISEE: Exactly. *(Realizing)* What?
SCRIBE *(reassuring)*: But that doesn't mean to say it was him.
PHARISEE: Couldn't have been.
SCRIBE: No, we weren't ready for him.
PHARISEE: Exactly.
BOTH: Well, you've really eased my mind... and yet...

(They both continue their business, go USL, take off props, collect props for PILATE *and* CAIAPHAS.*)*

NEWS SELLER: Read all about it. Jesus Alive. Friends in Confusion.

(5 as NICODEMUS *emerges SR, followed by 6 as* FRIEND *who catches him.)*

FRIEND: Nicodemus, have you heard?
NICODEMUS: Yes, I've heard. Strange news indeed. Yet it begins to make sense.
FRIEND: You surely don't believe? *(Pause.)* I mean, how can it be true?
NICODEMUS: It would explain so much. The words he spoke to me, they seemed riddles at the time. But now I begin to understand.
FRIEND: But if he really has risen—it means—*(pauses, as penny drops)* it means he was who he said he was.
NICODEMUS *(smiling)*: Do you still doubt that?

(They continue on their way. 3 and 4 go USL.)

NEWS SELLER: Read all about it. Jesus Lives. News Reaches Disciples.

(3 and 4 as PETER *and* MARY *enter together.)*

PETER: Mary, are you sure?
MARY: I've seen him, Peter.
PETER: Where?
MARY: Near where he was buried. He sent me to tell you.
PETER: He said he would rise from the dead. I never under-

stood before.

MARY: We must tell the others.

PETER: I can hardly believe it.

MARY: You must, Peter, you must.

PETER: But these last three days...

MARY: They're over. He's alive.

PETER: Yes. Yes, he is alive. Come on. Let's find the others.

(They rush off excitedly USL, to take off props.)

NEWS SELLER: Read all about it. Tomb Found Empty. Official enquiry called.

(PILATE and CAIAPHAS emerge from the crowd clearly troubled.)

PILATE: Well, what's this all about?

CAIAPHAS: A rumour, Pilate, that's all.

PILATE: So you still have the body secure?

CAIAPHAS: Well, no...

PILATE: I thought you were guarding it.

CAIAPHAS: We were, but...

PILATE: You fool. This is all your doing.

CAIAPHAS: The disciples must have pinched it and made up this story.

PILATE *(Sarcastically)*: Oh yes, just pushed a ten-ton stone aside when we weren't looking, I suppose.

CAIAPHAS: Well, no...but...

PILATE: So, this Province becomes ungovernable.

CAIAPHAS: What will you do?

PILATE: Me? Why should I do anything?

CAIAPHAS: But you had him killed.

PILATE: I've told you already. I wash my hands of the whole affair.

CAIAPHAS: It's not going to look that way in Rome, is it?

PILATE *(his nerve beginning to break)*: I only did it to appease the crowd.

CAIAPHAS: Well we must do something.

PILATE: We must stop these stupid rumours.

CAIAPHAS: How?

PILATE: Find the body.

CAIAPHAS: If there is one.

PILATE: What do you mean?

CAIAPHAS: I mean, what if? No it's nothing. But it won't be easy.

PILATE: Find it—or you'll have more than your reputation to lose.

(They move DSL with backs to audience.)

NEWS SELLER: Read all about it. Jesus Lives. Disciples Celebrate.

(Enter 3 and 4 as PETER *and* MARY *with 5 as* THOMAS *and 6 as a* DISCIPLE.*)*

THOMAS: I don't believe it.

MARY: But it's true I tell you.

THOMAS: But it's not possible. You must have imagined it.

PETER: Remember what he said, Thomas, 'In three days...'

THOMAS: Yes, I know all that. But I'll believe it when I see it.

MARY *(turning OS, her attention caught by something above audience)*: Look! *(All look.)*

PETER: Now's your chance, Thomas. *(*THOMAS *falls to his knees. All freeze.)*

NEWS SELLER: Good News. Read all about it. Death Defeated. Jesus Lives.

(The light falls on the TWO DARK FIGURES, *positioned to one side of the stage. 1 has his head in his hands. He appears exhausted, and defeated, after a long struggle. 1 and 2 turn.)*

1: I can't believe it.

2: What happened?

1: I had him. Here in my grasp. In my kingdom.

2: Then we've won.

1: No. Oh no. He got away.

2: Away? But how?

1: He slipped from my grasp. There was a struggle. He took the keys.

2: The keys?

1: Of imprisonment, possession, death. He destroyed our most powerful weapon of all. Just when I thought I had destroyed him—he still lives.

2: Then we've lost?

1: Ultimately yes—but there are still battles to win. *(Looks at audience.)* No, there is still one course left to us.

2: What?
1: We have to make people believe none of this ever really happened.

(They freeze and the lights begin to fade. The NEWS SELLER*'s voice is heard as the lights go down.)*

NEWS SELLER: Good news. Jesus Is Risen. Read all about it.

Wisdom of the Wise

A sketch about how God's wisdom is something far beyond human wisdom.

CHARACTERS: NIGEL, *a brilliant academic*
COLIN, *an even more brilliant academic*
GORDON, *a not quite so brilliant, but nevertheless fairly brilliant academic*

SCENE: NIGEL *and* COLIN *are sitting on a bench discussing the isness of reality, etc. We meet them as the conversation is in mid-flow.*

BOTH *(laughing)*: Ha! Ha! Ha! Quite so, quite so.
NIGEL: But tell me. How would you define the term, God?
COLIN: Ah, how indeed. I'm not sure that one can. I mean, I'm not exactly sure what you mean by the term 'define' exactly.
NIGEL: Well, I suppose in using the term 'define', one is trying to say, what sort of characteristics, er, er, attributes, and, if one might use the term strictly in its non-controversial sense, understanding, would you ascribe to the word, 'God'?
COLIN: Ah now I'm with you there. I suppose one could say that 'God' is in essence an indefinable, possibly infinite being, substance or form, that, or, who, may or may not exist in an indeterminable, or possibly quite determinable, though as yet, of course, undetermined, form and

that, or who, may, or may not, interact with that strange collection of atoms and molecules known as man, in a manner in conjunction with their perceptions of whatsoever he or she conceives him, her or it in essence to be.

NIGEL: Yes. I'm not sure I could say that.

COLIN: Well, I know it isn't easy, but I'm sure you could with practice.

NIGEL: No, I mean, I'm not sure that I'm quite at one with your definition, if I may describe it as such. I'm not entirely happy with the term, 'God is'. I mean, although I would wholeheartedly agree with the proposition that 'for God to be God he has to be God', I'm not entirely comfortable with the supposition that one can ascribe to God that term, 'is'.

COLIN: Yes. I suppose it depends on how one exactly defines the term, 'is', and whether one can relate its isness in proportion to the isness of God. I would tend to think that...

(Enter GORDON, *obviously excited, but also a little overawed.)*

GORDON: I've met him. I've met him.

NIGEL: Ah, Gordon. How did the lecture on the relevance of Buddha to the interaction of the frog and the milk jug go?

GORDON: I've met him. He actually spoke to me.

COLIN: Er, to what significant personage can you be said to have been inter-relating, Gordon?

GORDON: Him. The great I AM.

NIGEL: Can't say I know him. Is he one of your problem students?

GORDON: He isn't one of my students.

COLIN: Certainly isn't one of mine.

GORDON: No, you don't understand. I have just met with God.

NIGEL *(scratching head)*: Can one meet with God?

COLIN: To entertain such a possibility would certainly necessitate an element of reassessment of one's definition.

GORDON: But you must listen. I've just made an amazing discovery. God is alive. God is real.

NIGEL: Did you hear that?

COLIN: Amazing.

GORDON: At last I'm getting through.

NIGEL: He actually said, 'God is' twice and didn't bat an eyelid.

COLIN: Gordon, I feel we ought to tell you that we're not quite at one with the term, 'God is'. Perhaps you could rephrase it for us.

GORDON: How can I rephrase it? It's true. I've just met him right in my room. I was studying the Gospels…

NIGEL: Gospels?

COLIN: You know. The synoptic portraits of the life of Jesus. Matthew, Mark and Luke. We sometimes touch on them with the first years.

NIGEL: Of course.

GORDON: And I was just reading the Gospel of John.

COLIN & NIGEL *(disapprovingly)*: Ah. But John's another Gospel. *(They nod to one another, knowingly.)*

GORDON: And there seemed to be so many verses that challenged the theses of my book, *The myth of Christ as Son of God*.

NIGEL: A brilliant work if I may say so, Gordon.

COLIN: So deep, so profound.

GORDON: I was so disturbed by what I was reading, that I did something I have never done before.

COLIN & NIGEL *(shocked gasps)*: You gave one of your students an 'A'.

GORDON: I cried out to God for understanding.

COLIN & NIGEL: Oh, that's all right then. *(Shocked.)* You did what?

NIGEL: Can one, er, cry out to God?

COLIN: Well, I always think it depends on what one means when one uses the term 'to cry out to God'. Certainly there is evidence that those who possess some kind of faith, whatsoever one might conceive faith to be, have been known to cry out to a deity that they might refer to as God, but it's not the sort of thing I would expect from anyone as intelligent as Gordon.

GORDON *(startling them)*: Quite suddenly, the room was filled with the presence of God.

NIGEL: Doesn't that presuppose that the presence of God is something much larger than, and far beyond the scope of, human understanding?

COLIN: Nothing is beyond the scope of my understanding.

GORDON: I fell on my knees. I never realized he was so...so vast, so powerful. After all these years studying about him, to meet him so suddenly was—amazing.

NIGEL *(to Colin)*: Would you concur with my proposition that Gordon appears to have experienced some sort of religious experience?

COLIN: A close encounter of the supernatural kind. I say, that's quite good. I must use it in my next lecture.

GORDON: Then—he spoke to me.

NIGEL: A God who communicates? Interesting concept.

COLIN: Profoundly disturbing.

GORDON: His voice was so clear. It had such authority.

NIGEL: Now, come along, Gordon. Surely if such a divine form could be said to exist, so to speak, and if it did wish to communicate, would it not come first to the head of department instead of some mere junior tutor. You haven't even got a Ph.D.

GORDON: I can't explain it. All I know is that he filled my room with his presence and spoke to me. What he said came as quite a shock, too. *(Pauses as if pondering on what God has just said to him.)*

NIGEL & COLIN *(impatiently)*: Well?

GORDON: What? Oh, he said, 'I am the Lord your God, and I will destroy the wisdom of the wise; the intelligence of the intelligent I will frustrate. For my foolishness is wiser than man's wisdom, and my weakness is stronger than man's strength.'

NIGEL & COLIN *(digesting this, disturbed)*: Oh.

NIGEL: Interesting concept. *(Sounding a little less certain.)*

COLIN: Profoundly disturbing. *(Regaining confidence.)* Er, did he say how he'd define wisdom?

GORDON: For since in its wisdom the world did not know me, I have chosen the foolish things to shame the wise, the weak to shame the strong and the lowly to humble the great.

(Stunned silence.)

NIGEL: No, er, surely you've got all that the wrong way round. Didn't he say anything about the importance of knowledge?

COLIN: Or about the clever leading the way?

GORDON: No, but he did say something about the message of the cross which was regarded as foolishness by many, being the power of life to those who believe. My head was spinning, I can tell you. And then, I felt a hand gently touch me, and I heard someone say, 'I love you.' I turned, and there he was, holding out his arms to me.

NIGEL & COLIN *(perplexed)*: Who?

GORDON: Jesus.

NIGEL: Jesus, in your room? Oh don't be silly, Gordon.

COLIN: Did you ask him whether he had an eschatologically orientated self-consciousness?

GORDON: I didn't have to ask him anything. As soon as I saw him I knew that this man is the Son of God.

COLIN: Son of God? Oh no, quite impossible. *(Horror stricken.)* I'd have to rewrite my book.

GORDON: I've already torn mine up.

NIGEL *(mortified)*: But you can't do that.

COLIN: Such a brilliant scholarly work.

GORDON: But it was wrong! It's such an amazing feeling to know that Jesus is alive and he cares about me. A chance to start again without having to spend the rest of my life going round in circles wondering what the point is.

NIGEL: What does he mean by 'point'?

COLIN: A point is a sharp outer extremity at the end of an object, but I don't see what that has to do with it. Now look, Gordon, you must understand that no self-respecting, intelligent man in your position can believe about God and things.

GORDON: Well, if we can't believe in him, why do we study him anyway?

NIGEL & COLIN *(floundering)*: Well, er, er, er, *(Smugly, together.)* To search for deeper truths.

GORDON: I've found the truth.

COLIN *(as* GORDON *starts to exit, excitedly)*: Er, no, Gordon. The truth isn't something one finds, it's something one searches for. Where are you going?

GORDON: To tell somebody. *(Exits)*

NIGEL: Gordon, come back. You can't go around telling people about this sort of thing....

COLIN: Poor chap. Never mind, I expect he'll get over it.

NIGEL: Yes, I suppose so. But tell me, *(as they walk off)* how would you explain Gordon's experience?

COLIN: Well, I think that depends on how one defines the term 'Gordon'.

Pulling a Fast One

A sketch about God's chosen Fast. Taken from Isaiah 58.

CHARACTERS: A *and* B, *two fairly well off, flamboyantly dressed, greedy hypocrites*
THE PROPHET
THE OPPRESSED, *a worker, a hungry person, an ill clad person, a homeless person and a 2nd hungry person.*

SCENE: *An empty stage. Enter* A, *carrying bags full of food and eating a cream doughnut. From the other side a* WORKER *enters.*

A: You there! What are you doing away from your work-bench?

WORKER: Excuse me, sir. *(Doffs cap, respectfully.)* I was just coming to see you about my wages.

A: Wages? Who said anything about wages? Now get back to work. *(Pushes worker away to other side of stage. Sits down, surrounded by bags of food and begins to pray, piously.)* Dear Father God, I thank thee that I am not like other men. *(Enter* HUNGRY MAN.*)* I seek thee every day, O Lord...

HUNGRY PERSON: Excuse me, sir.

A: Go away. Can't you see I'm praying?

HUNGRY PERSON: Sorry, sir. But I was wondering if you might be able to help me.

A: Of course, my dear chap. I'll say a prayer for you.

HUNGRY PERSON: Thank you, sir. But could you spare me something to eat as well?

A: To eat? Er, well. *(Looks round at his food bags.)* I seem to be a bit low on food at the moment. Perhaps some other time.

*(*HUNGRY PERSON *shuffles to side of stage and joins Worker.)*

A *(continuing prayer)*: I thank you for your many blessings, Lord, and pray *(looks at food)* that I may continue to enjoy them. *(Looks at food again, longingly, and then resumes praying posture.)* Lord... *(Does the same again.)* Lord, you are... *(Takes another look.)* Oh Lord... *(Takes another look, and then finally gives in.)* For what I am about to receive, etc, etc, Amen.

(Grabs food and starts stuffing it in.)

(Enter B, *also eating. He sees* A *and hurriedly puts food in pocket.* A *sees* B *and also tries to hide the food. Stands up to greet* B.*)*

B: Hello there. Good to see you. Would you like one of these new peppermints?

A *(tries to say 'No' but it is muffled by the fact that his mouth is full. Finally manages to speak)*: No thank you. *(Picking his teeth.)* I'm fasting.

B: That's funny, so am I. I only bought these to give to you. But as you're fasting you won't want them, will you?

A: I, er... *(Watches with pained expression as* B *puts sweets back in pocket.)* Well, I suppose not.

B: I say, have you noticed how slim I'm looking? I've been fasting for three whole days now.

A: Really? It's just as well you had such a vast amount of fat resources to live on then, isn't it? *(*B *looks hurt.)* Anyway, one does not fast to lose weight. One fasts to be closer to God and to seek his will.

B: Oh yes, of course. I heard you praying.

A *(looking pious)*: Did you?

B: Very eloquent, if I may say so. *(*A *looks even more pious.)*

You must have been practising.

A *(haughtily)*: If you mean I must have been doing a lot of praying recently, then I must admit that although one doesn't like to appear superspiritual one has spent a lot of time on one's knees lately.

B: Hmm. Did you manage to find that contact lens you dropped?

A: Ha! Ha! Very witty. *(Enter* ILL CLAD PERSON, *shivering.)*

B: Look out. Here comes a dedicated follower of fashion.

*(*ILL CLAD PERSON *shuffles past them and joins Worker and Hungry Person on other side of stage.)*

A: Actually, I don't mind admitting that I'm finding it very hard to fast at the moment.

*(*HOMELESS PERSON *is pushed on to the stage.)*

HOMELESS PERSON *(to person off)*: No, you can't throw me out. I've nowhere to go.

A: I mean, it seems to me we spend all this time humbling ourselves before God, fasting and praying, and he doesn't seem to be answering.

*(*HOMELESS PERSON, *completely ignored by* A *and* B, *gets up and joins others on side of stage.)*

B: Yes, I know what you mean. Not that I mind a bit of good old sacrifice.

A: No, of course.

B: All the same, one would like to feel that it achieved something.

(Enter PROPHET.*)*

A: I sometimes think he doesn't notice.

B: Yes, I mean, what do we have to do?

PROPHET *(loudly, standing behind them)*: Shout it aloud. Do not hold back.

*(*A *and* B *jump, startled.)*

A: I say, old chap, steady on. Nearly blew my ear off.

PROPHET: The Lord says, 'Raise your voice like a trumpet. Declare to my people their rebellion.'

B: Jolly good. Off you go then.

A: Yes. About time, I say. I saw some very rebellious people on my way to the prayer meeting this morning.

*(*PROPHET *remains unmoved.)*

B: What's he looking at us like that for?

A: He can't mean...?*(Turns to Prophet.)* You surely can't mean us?

PROPHET: You're the ones.

B: How dare you, sir. Haven't you seen the way we've been fasting and praying?

PROPHET: Yes, I've seen you all right. You may seem eager enough to hear God's voice, but on the day of your fasting you do exactly as you please. You exploit your workers.

A: Now look here, just who do you think...?

PROPHET: You quarrel over who's fasted the longest, who's the most pious.

B: I would certainly never say anything rude about my friend here. I mean, he's had his spiritual ups and downs, but he's trying very hard to reform himself.

A: Just what do you mean by that?

PROPHET: There you go again, you see. You can't fast as you are doing and expect your voice to be heard. Is this what you call a fast acceptable to God? Look, you wanted to hear from him. Come over here and listen to what he has to say to you.

(He takes them over to the other side of the stage where those that A *and* B *rejected are huddled in dejection, pain and poverty. If there is lighting available, this side of the stage could be in darkness until the* PROPHET *takes* A *and* B *over to it. The* PROPHET *leads* A *and* B *among the dejected figures.)*

Is not this the kind of fasting I choose? To loose the chains of injustice, to untie the cords of the yoke, and to set the oppressed free. *(As he speaks he helps up the Worker and frees him from his imaginary chains. The* WORKER *exits joyfully.)* And to break every yoke? Is it not to share your food with the hungry? *(Takes food from* A *and gives it to* HUNGRY PERSON. *Nods to* A *and encourages him to do the same.* A *does so, reluctantly at first, but finding it easier has he goes among the others. He is surprised by the joyful response of each person.)* Is it not to provide the poor wanderer with shelter? *(Helps up* HOMELESS PERSON *and leads to side of stage, points.* HOMELESS PERSON *exits gratefully.)* To clothe the naked when you see him *(*A *prods* B *who sees* ILL CLAD PERSON *and gives him his* *coat, reluctantly.* ILL CLAD PERSON *shakes him enthusiastically by the hand.)* and not to turn away from your own flesh and blood? Then your light will break forth like the dawn, and your healing will quickly appear. Your righteousness will go before you and the glory of the Lord will be your rearguard. Then you will call and the Lord will answer. You will cry for help and he will say, Here am I.

(As the last person is helped up and exits, the PROPHET *moves away leaving* A *and* B *to reflect on what they have seen.)*

A: I've never seen it like that before.

B *(angrily)*: Who does he think he is to talk like that?

A: B-but he's right, isn't he?

B: Right? But he's just called us hypocrites.

A: But didn't you see them? Didn't you see the way they were, and the way they were so excited and grateful when we helped them? Didn't you feel different?

B: Well, I—er Oh, I don't want to talk about it. Let's go and have lunch.

A: No, no. I don't feel hungry. I've got to go away and think about this.

B: Come on, old man, don't take it to heart.

A: I'll see you later. *(Exits quickly, leaving* B *standing alone.* B *picks up some of the left-over food and takes a bite.)*

(Enter 2ND HUNGRY PERSON.*)*

2ND HUNGRY PERSON: Excuse me. I don't suppose you could spare me a little of that could you?

B: No, I could not. *(He starts to exit, passing* 2ND HUNGRY PERSON. *Turns, looks at* 2ND HUNGRY PERSON *who looks back at him, almost pleadingly. Both freeze.)*

PROPHET: If you do away with the yoke of oppression, with the pointing finger and malicious talk, and if you spend yourselves on behalf of the hungry, and satisfy the needs of the oppressed, then your light will shine in the darkness and your night will become like the noonday. The Lord will guide you always. He will satisfy your needs in a sun-scorched land and strengthen you. You will be like a spring whose waters never fail.

SECTION 2

by

Andy Kelso

A Word from the Author

The scripts included here are the result of five years of writing and directing for the Domini Theatre Group, and all of them have been tried and tested in a variety of situations, from the grandeur of the Royal Albert Hall to a windswept hillside in Kent, from the Central Hall, Westminster to a tiny church in Shepperton.

As regards numbers there are scripts for one character and scripts for twenty-one, but you will find that most of them can be adapted to the number in your group.

Each script has some directional notes, to be ignored by those with more positive ideas, and to be used as a starting point for others. If you have no access to spotlighting you can always highlight a character by bringing him into the foreground, or standing him on a box. Improvisation is a good spark to creativity.

All manner of styles of presentation are evident, and all types of mood are represented. The important point with regard to them all is the need for a crispness in presentation.

The uses of these scripts are many and various—theatre presentations, schools, churches and street theatre. Ideas for presentations are noted as well as ways of linking material together.

I hope that those of you who tackle these scripts gain as much enjoyment from them as I did in writing and producing them. It does not matter whether your 'Albert Hall' is your church hall or school hall. What does matter is that you enjoy the experience, gain from it, and share it.

Andy Kelso

The Parable of the Prodigal Son

CHARACTERS: NARRATOR
Eight ACTORS

(Note: A piece for eight actors, less if you double up. All props can be mimed or real. If used as an outdoor piece then colourful props are useful, along with suggested alternative pig episode! This is ideal with a follow-up talk on the fatherly nature of God.)

SCENE: *Three* ACTORS *stand side by side, backs to audience.* NARRATOR *stands DSR at the lectern.* NARRATOR *opens Bible.*

NARRATOR: There was once a man *(Middle* ACTOR *turns to face audience and becomes* FATHER.*)* who had two sons. *(*FATHER *opens out arms to indicate his* SONS.*)* An elder son *(*SON *SL turns around, looking pleased with himself somewhat distanced from the* FATHER *shown by self-righteous look.)* who worked hard on the estate and was very dutiful *(*FATHER *goes to put arm around him.* SON *turns gesture into a polite handshake.)* and a younger son *(*SON *SR turns around sulkily.)* who was lazy and self-centred and caused great heartache to his father. *(*YOUNGER SON *has his hands in his pockets and looks generally bad-tempered. His back is half turned away from* FATHER, *who looks at this* SON *with sorrow, reaching out to him. The* ELDER SON *shakes his head disdainfully.)* The younger son said to his father

YOUNGER SON: *(Turning to* FATHER*)* I want my share of your wealth now! *(*FATHER *looks at* SONS *sadly. Takes out cheque book, writes a cheque and gives it to* YOUNGER SON. *He looks in amazement at the cheque, then looks very self-satisfied and greedy. The* ELDER SON *folds his arms disdainfully.)*

NARRATOR: A few days later *(All three* ACTORS *move around the area, interweaving; the* FATHER *looking sorrowful, the* ELDER SON *looking disdainful, the* YOUNGER SON *looking jubilant—holding up the cheque. They return to their places.)* the younger son packed up all his things *(The* YOUNGER SON *moves off SR to collect and bring back a suitcase.)* and left for a distant land. *(*YOUNGER SON *kisses the cheque and disappears through audience with his suitcase, with a wave, but doesn't look back.* ELDER SON *exits SL with self-satisfied smile, while* FATHER *looks sadly after* YOUNGER SON *then goes to a higher level e.g. pulpit or step-ladder USL to watch him disappear.* FATHER *then exits SL.)*

When he got there *(Three or more* ACTORS *enter the area. They take up a freeze tableau of gambling, covering as much of centre stage as possible. No furniture or props are needed, but they can be used.* ACTOR *1 has his arm around* ACTOR *2.* ACTOR *3 is drinking from a bottle,* ACTOR *4 is dealing cards. Other* ACTORS *can be gambling, serving drinks, etc.* YOUNGER SON *hurries through the audience, with suitcase, stops at the front, looks at the imaginary sign, grins at audience and enters. The group break their freeze, and mime appropriately to their character. The* ACTORS *stop in unison and look at* YOUNGER SON. *He looks sheepish.* ACTORS *wink and nudge each other knowingly.)* he wasted all his money *(*YOUNGER SON *draws out a roll of notes.* ACTORS *greet him fawningly.)* on drink, *(He is proffered a glass by* ACTORS, *downs it, is offered another and downs it, and a third. He gives two or three notes to* ACTOR *2 who tucks them down her front. She fawns over him.)* gambling *(*YOUNGER SON *throws down three or four notes and beckons for cards which are dealt with knowing looks. He throws down more notes as* ACTOR *4 lays down his cards.* YOUNGER SON *throws down his cards in despair as* ACTOR *4 slyly pools the takings.)* and reckless living *(The same routines of drink, gambling, etc. are played out, getting faster.)* until he had nothing left. *(His suitcase, jacket, tie, hat are taken.)*

*(*YOUNGER SON *looks for another drink, another set of cards, etc. but first* ACTOR *3 turns away showing rejection, then* ACTOR *2, then the others. He pleads wildly. The* ACTORS *turn and grabbing him they propel him DSC. The group pick up his suitcase*

and exit smiling and counting his money. As they do so FATHER *appears in the pulpit or on the step-ladder, looking out, then exits.)* Then a great famine swept across the land and he began to starve. *(*YOUNGER SON *picks himself up off 'the street', and becomes a street beggar, begging to the audience.)*

Finally, he hired himself out to a local farmer *(Two* ACTORS *enter SR. The* YOUNGER SON *pleads with them on his knees. They smile at each other, and one of them picks him up roughly and sends him off pointing to his fields, SL.* YOUNGER SON *exits SL. One* ACTOR *exits after him, the other* ACTOR *exits SR.)*

He was sent into the fields to feed the pigs. *(*YOUNGER SON *enters SR carrying a bucket of slop which he pours into the trough. He wipes his brow.)* He became so hungry that even the pigswill looked good to him. *(*YOUNGER SON *suddenly kneels and gets handfuls of slop and feeds himself.)*

* * *

ALTERNATIVE PIG EPISODE

(The pigs appear with the two ACTORS*, grunting. They nose and prod at* YOUNGER SON*, rather like unruly children. He then has to chase after them when the* FARMER *points to the fields. After the group exit, and* NARRATOR'S *line: 'He was sent into the fields to feed the pigs,'* YOUNGER SON *enters with* PIGS*, carrying a bucket of slop. He looks into bucket, then at audience, indicating that it is revolting. So do the* PIGS*. He finally pours it into the trough, averting his head. The* PIGS *nose up to it, but turn away disgustedly.)*

NARRATOR: He became hungry. *(*YOUNGER SON *holds stomach, looks at slop as if contemplating eating it—then shakes head. So do the* PIGS*.)*

He then became *very* hungry. *(*YOUNGER SON *repeats the process, but with longer consideration.* PIGS *look puzzled at each other and at audience.)*

And finally he became *very, very* hungry. *(*YOUNGER SON *looks at* PIGS *and then audience with a 'What else can I do?' look and dives into trough. The* PIGS *are open-mouthed, and, grunting* *loudly, they go to join him, as he consumes handfuls of slop. The* PIGS *can take no more and exit SR.)*

* * *

NARRATOR: Finally he came to his senses and said

YOUNGER SON: *(looking up slowly he wipes his hands on his clothes.)* Here am I starving, while my father's workers have food to spare! *(He slowly gets up.)* I'll go home...and I'll say: 'Father... I'm sorry... I was in the wrong. I know I'm not worthy to be treated like a son any more—that I've brought shame on the family—but please, please take me back, as one of your workers.'

*(*YOUNGER SON *slowly walks down through the audience, head bowed. If bucket and trough have actually been used then the two* ACTORS *who were farmers clear the area.* FATHER *climbs on the step-ladder or into the pulpit.)*

NARRATOR: And so it was that he returned home.

*(*YOUNGER SON *having got to the back of the audience comes the other way now.* FATHER *sights him, hurries down from the level and calls* ELDER SON *who enters SL. They talk together, the* FATHER *pointing in the direction of the* YOUNGER SON.*)*

But when he arrived, no one wanted anything to do with him. *(*FATHER'S *expression has suddenly changed, as he turns to meet* YOUNGER SON. *He looks stern and unforgiving.* ELDER SON *smirks.)*

YOUNGER SON: Father... I....

FATHER: Clear off! How dare you think you can come back here, you worthless layabout!

ELDER SON: You heard! Shove off. You got what you deserved! *(He pushes* YOUNGER SON *away.* NARRATOR *closes Bible with finality.* FATHER *and* ELDER SON *turn their backs to* YOUNGER SON. *Silence.)*

PERSON: *(In audience—flustered—as if really interrupting.)* But ... that's not what it says. *(*NARRATOR *looks up.* ACTORS *turn to look at this* PERSON.*)* That's not how it ends. You've... you've missed the whole point!

NARRATOR: Well, he got what he deserved, didn't he?

PERSON: But that's just it. He *didn't* get what he deserved because it's all about forgiveness and God's love.

NARRATOR: Well go on then. You finish it off. Let's see *your* ending.

*(*PERSON *comes up somewhat shyly, and takes the Bible.* NARRATOR *stands to one side.* ACTORS *have resumed their positions:* YOUNGER SON *at back of audience,* FATHER *on level looking out,* ELDER SON *offstage.)*

PERSON: And so it was that he returned home. *(*YOUNGER SON *starts down through the audience.* FATHER *sights him, his face lights up, and he hurries down from the level.)* But while he was still a long way away, his father saw him coming, and filled as he was with love for his son, and sadness at his condition, he ran to meet him. *(*FATHER *hurries down and embraces* YOUNGER SON.*)*

YOUNGER SON: Father...I...I'm sorry.

FATHER: My son, my son! *(Leading him home. They freeze.)*

NARRATOR: Oh come on! This is ridiculous! You're not telling me the father's as daft as that are you? The son took him for all he was worth. He'll probably try the same thing again. What kind of idiot father are you suggesting?

PERSON: *(closing Bible)* The kind that's shown here *(pointing to Bible)*. A Father God of love, of forgiveness. A Father God who never gives up on us.

NARRATOR: But that kind of God is...well....

PERSON: Yes! A God who gambles!

(Freeze. Hold for five seconds. Break freeze. PERSON *walks back to seat.* FATHER, SON, NARRATOR *exit.)*

The Parable of the Sower

CHARACTERS: NARRATOR
Seven ACTORS (or more)

Notes:
1. See note at the end of 'The Parable of the Good Samaritan' as to ideas for linking the two pieces.
2. Because there is quite a lot of low-level acting, it would be useful if the acting area was raised somehow.
3. This is a piece that works well both indoors and out. If doing it outdoors more colour is needed, so let the FARMER *wear straw hat, braces, etc.; the seed wear yellow T-shirts, and colourful socks; and the group who represent birds, rocks and thorns, wear something appropriate for each e.g. children's Indian headdress, or black cloaks for birds, basic black for rocks, and ghoulish masks for thorns.*
4. A NARRATOR *enters to stand DR. A line of* ACTORS *enter to stand side by side, centre stage, their heads hanging down as if asleep. Dressed in black.*

NARRATOR: Listen! *(The* ACTORS *jerk awake. They start groaning and mumbling.)* Listen! A farmer decided to sow some seed. *(A central* ACTOR *moves DSC pulls imaginary braces and scratches head. On pulling the braces the group say 'ooohh' and when he lets go painfully they say 'aahh'. They giggle and the* NARRATOR *coughs.)*
Act one.

ALL: The path.

NARRATOR: Some of it fell on a path. *(*FARMER *mimes this, sowing from panniers at side. The* ACTORS *on one side of him roll into area as 'seed' curled up into tight individual positions. The* FARMER *steps back into line.)* But the birds came and ate it all up. *(The* ACTORS *on the other side of* FARMER *become crows,* *squawking and flapping arms. Lots of arm and hand movement and good expressive use of face are needed. They alight above a seed. The seed pleads for its life. The crows pick up the seed. The* NARRATOR *claps. All freeze and then return to line.* ACTORS *excitedly congratulate themselves in their acting.* NARRATOR *coughs. All stand still.)*

Act two.

ALL: The rocks.

NARRATOR: Some fell on rocky ground with poor soil. *(The* FARMER *steps forward and sows on another area. Those who were the birds become rocks, then the 'seed'* ACTORS *roll among the 'rocks'.)*

They sprang up quickly enough, but there was little root. *(The seed springs up in about four definite stages of growth, sharply and in unison.)* And they soon withered under the hot, burning sun…and died. *(The seed slowly withers to the ground, showing thirst, etc. With the words 'and died' the* NARRATOR *claps. They all return to line, excited, as before.* NARRATOR *coughs. Silence.)*

Act three.

ALL: The thorns.

NARRATOR: Some seed fell among thorns. *(*FARMER *steps forward and sows the 'seed'. They roll into area together.)* The seeds grew up well enough, *(Seeds grow up to three quarters of full height.)* but so did the thorns. *(The thorns grow quickly and tower over seeds. Lots of angles. Each thorn takes one seed and has a different way of strangling its seed. The thorns enjoy the massacre and take obvious pleasure in the victory.)* And they produced nothing. *(All the thorns hold a victory pose above their victim, arm raised, one foot on victim. The* NARRATOR *claps. They return to line, all excited.* NARRATOR *coughs, exasperated.)*

Act four.

ALL: The good soil.

NARRATOR: But some of the seed fell into good soil. *(*FARMER *steps forward and sows. The others form 'furrows' lying US to DS. The 'seed' rolls into these.)* It yielded grain. *(The seed slowly rises.)* Thirty… *(One of the 'furrows' rises to become seed.)* sixty… *(Two or three of the 'furrows' rise.)* and even 180 times as much as was planted. *('180' said like a darts* *commentator. Three or more of the furrows rise. The* ACTORS *sway together as corn in a field. They have happy faces.* NARRATOR *claps. Return to line. Very excited. Exasperated, the* NARRATOR *brings out a whistle and blows it.* ACTORS *are shocked into stillness.)*

If you have ears....

GROUP: Corny!

NARRATOR: *(looking daggers at them)* If you have ears... *(*ACTORS *step forward on right leg, holding right hand cupped to right ear.)* Then listen! *(*ACTORS *step back, in turn, and drop their heads. Same positions as at the beginning.)*

The Parable of the Good Samaritan

CHARACTERS: NARRATOR
Eight ACTORS (or more)

Notes:

1. The NARRATOR *could be adapted for two parts. One supplies the narrative, while the other provides the various voices i.e. says all the speech. One* NARRATOR *would therefore need to use different accents for the characters. One* NARRATOR *would stand DSL the other DSR.*

2. The different characters can have one prop/costume to help distinguish them from the rest e.g. TEACHER *has a heavy book,* PRIEST *has a dog collar or long gown,* LEVITE *has large cross,* SAMARITAN *has a flat cap,* INN KEEPER *has apron,* INJURED MAN *has head bandage with red on it, but first appears with colourful cloak,* JESUS *has a simple jerkin. All of the* ACTORS *could have a basic colour e.g. black, over which they wear an item.*

3. Vocal effects by the ACTORS *are most necessary—easier than music because of technical difficulties and they give more creative scope. Those left offstage create these effects.*

4. References to the SAMARITAN *as male are not intended to exclude women from playing this role.*

5. Use simple props where possible e.g. in the bandaging scene, in the

robbery scene, in the inn scene.
6. Miming the mule, throwing the body over the mule etc. is not easy, so if necessary use an actor! However, the piece does require exaggerated mime from everybody, with the characters responding to the NARRATOR(S).

SCENE: *A group of* ACTORS *come into the area and form a grouping around one of them who represents* JESUS.

NARRATOR: A teacher of the Law came up and tried to trap Jesus.

(An ACTOR *appears SL, very proud of bearing. The* DISCIPLES *point at him in horror and then all hurriedly hide behind* JESUS. *Both the* TEACHER *and* JESUS *mime their dialogue.)*

(Very haughtily.) 'Teacher. What must I do to receive eternal life?'

(The DISCIPLES *all look at one another, hands over mouths, scratching heads, looking very puzzled.)*

Jesus answered him, 'What do the Scriptures say? How do you interpret them?'

(The DISCIPLES *all nod their heads looking terribly pleased, mime clapping, and then look intently at the* TEACHER.*)*

The man answered, 'Love the Lord your God with all your heart, with all your soul, with all your strength, and with all your mind.'

(The DISCIPLES *'tick' each area off on their fingers. They all nod among themselves at the end but then look up sharply and stare intently at the* TEACHER, *all tapping their last finger since he's missed something out.)*

'And love your neighbour as yourself.'

(All the DISCIPLES *nod, mime clapping and shake the* TEACHER*'s hand energetically.)*

'You are right,' Jesus replied. 'Do this and you will live.'

(The DISCIPLES *nod and point the* TEACHER *out.)*

But the teacher of the Law wanted to justify himself, so he asked Jesus, 'Who is my neighbour?'

(The TEACHER *had turned to go but then stops and returns over this. The* DISCIPLES *once again look puzzled, hold their fingers up to show the* TEACHER *has a good point and look at* JESUS. JESUS *gently beckons one half of the group to go to one side and*

the other to go to the other side. He then beckons the TEACHER *to come upstage with him thus leaving the area free.)*

Jesus answered, 'There was once a man,

(One of the group SR hurry onto the area and wave, pointing at himself. He is hauled back by the others.)

Who was going down from Jerusalem to Jericho.

(The MAN *enters mime-riding a mule across the area. Rest of the group make appropriate vocal hoof noises. Half way across the area the mule stops and snorts. Sound effects must stop when mule does. The* MAN *dismounts and tries to pull the mule with no success. He tries to push it. No success. He wipes the sweat off his brow and attempts to tell the mule off.)*

When a band of robbers...

(Three ROBBERS *appear SL with appropriate vocal effects, e.g. Pink Panther theme. They exaggerate pulling cloaks over their faces and then with comic mincing footsteps come up behind the* MAN.*)*

...attacked him...

*(*ROBBER *1 hits him over the head, and the* INJURED MAN *is knocked out and falls back, to be caught by* ROBBERS *2 and 3, and laid on the ground.)*

...stripped him...

(All three ROBBERS *make a large sweeping movement as if removing all his clothes, making sure they do remove his cloak.)*

...and beat him up...

(The ROBBERS *stop still and then slowly turn to the* NARRATOR.*)*

...and beat him up...

(They look at one another and smile, and then exaggeratedly 'put the boot in'.)

...leaving him half dead.

(The ROBBERS *stop, clap their hands over their mouths, looking worried. They try to revive the man, slapping his face, etc. and the* INJURED MAN *stirs a little. They look relieved and then tiptoe off, SR, with cloaks over faces with the same vocal effects. The* INJURED MAN *desperately tries to reach after them and then falls back.)*

It so happened that a priest was going down that road,

*(*PRIEST *enters SR with hands together in prayer and head tilted*

upwards. His bearing is extremely proud. Appropriate solemn, churchy vocal effects.) but when he saw the man...

he walked on by, on the other side.

(The PRIEST *takes two paces to his right and then continues his pious walk. As he reaches the other side he trips and regaining his bearing looks scornfully at the audience and continues.)*

In the same way another religious leader came along...

*(*LEVITE *figure enters SR in exactly the same way, with the same vocal effects.)*

...Went over and looked at the man...

*(*LEVITE *peers at the* INJURED MAN *from a distance.)*

He then walked on by on the other side.

*(*LEVITE *steps sideways across the body two paces and then continues his pious walk. Again, he trips like the* PRIEST *and scornfully looks at the audience. The pious music effects continue throughout.)*

But a Samaritan...

(A figure appears SR. ACTORS *boo and hiss.* SAMARITAN *looks downcast.)*

Who was travelling that way...

*(*SAMARITAN *rides in to appropriate vocal effects.)*

...Came upon the man.

(The SAMARITAN*'s mule suddenly stops when it hits the* INJURED MAN. *Appropriate vocal effects.* SAMARITAN *is propelled off the mule.)*

When he saw him...

*(*SAMARITAN, *picking himself up, notices the* INJURED MAN.*)*

His heart was filled with pity.

(The SAMARITAN *holds his hand to his heart. The group all vocalize sympathy: 'Ahhh...')*

He went over to him,

*(*SAMARITAN *edges away from the body as if trying to pretend he's not really moving. Then he suddenly strides back to* INJURED MAN.*)*

Poured oil and wine on his wounds.

(He mimes getting out a flask which he unstops and pours liberally over INJURED MAN. *Then he pulls out another flask and does similarly, pouring up and down the body, getting quite carried away.)*

And bandaged them.

(He lifts up a leg of the injured man which then stays upright and he mimes bandaging it. As he lowers the leg the other leg lifts up. This is repeated for arms and head.)

Then he put the man on his own mule,

(He attempts to lift the man up and fails a couple of times. He flexes his muscles and strains to lift him up, gets an arm around his shoulder and turning his back to the audience then throws the INJURED MAN *over the mule, so that his body hangs over it.* SAMARITAN *brushes his hands and then attempts to pull the mule which refuses to move. After several vain attempts the* SAMARITAN *moves to the rear and gives him a massive slap. The animal races off, with the* INJURED MAN *moving sideways at speed, and* SAMARITAN, *aghast, rushing after them.)*

(Rushed.) And took him to a nearby inn where he took care of him. *(Slowly again.)* The next day…

*(*ACTORS *rush on to either side and hold positions still.* INJURED MAN *is helped on SL by another.* SAMARITAN *enters with the* INNKEEPER. *Other* ACTORS *appear at the other side.)*

He took out two silver coins…

*(*SAMARITAN *deliberately pulls out two coins and holds them up.* ACTORS *look on longingly.)*

And gave them…

*(*ACTORS *crane forward expectantly.)*

(Quickly.) To the innkeeper.

*(*INNKEEPER *takes them and acknowledges his triumph to the audience. The other* DISCIPLES *look dejected.)*

'Take care of him' he told the innkeeper, 'and when I come back this way, I will pay you whatever else you spend on him.'

*(*SAMARITAN *turns to exit SR.* INNKEEPER *smiles, taps his nose and winks at the audience. He taps* SAMARITAN *on the shoulder and shakes his head at the two coins. He turns holding his hand out behind.* SAMARITAN *pulls out some more money.* INNKEEPER *quickly looks at it, shows the audience he's going to get more and then turns to beckon more money into his palm.* SAMARITAN *reluctantly does so.* SAMARITAN *and* ACTORS *exit.* INNKEEPER *looks at the money and then rushes off excitedly.* INJURED MAN *and* HELPER *reach out after him and*

attempt to follow.)

And Jesus concluded.

*(*ACTORS *rush onto the area and group around* JESUS *and the* TEACHER.*)*

'In your opinion... *(they all look terribly important)* which one of these three...

*(*PRIEST, LEVITE *and* SAMARITAN, *in turn, stand up and come down to the front of the area and then walk across as if in a modelling competition or Mr Universe.* PRIEST *models first, then* LEVITE *and then* SAMARITAN.*)*

Which one of these three acted like a neighbour towards the man attacked by the robbers?'

*(*INJURED MAN *comes DS on the other side from the models, on crutches.)*

The teacher of the Law answered

(The TEACHER *is about to answer when all the* DISCIPLES *turn on him and mime for him to be quiet. One of them puts his hand over the man's mouth. Then all the* DISCIPLES *gather in a circle, arms around shoulders, and then huddle down whispering loudly as to who they think. On the first huddle some say 'Priest' and some say 'Levite'. Then they all come up for air and look in unison first at* PRIEST, *then at* LEVITE. *On the last huddle they all come to agreement on* SAMARITAN *and* SAMARITAN *is propelled out to the other side, looking somewhat dazed.* ACTORS *go down on one knee with arms reaching out towards* SAMARITAN.*)*

(Bad temperedly.) 'The one who was kind to him!'

*(*TEACHER *looks very put out.* DISCIPLES *look very pleased with themselves, congratulate one another, polish their halos, etc.* SAMARITAN *raises arms in triumph.)*

Jesus replied, 'Now you go and do the same.'

*(*DISCIPLES *beckon to* TEACHER, *and all point SR.* TEACHER *exits rather shamefacedly.* DISCIPLES *look very pleased with themselves, until* JESUS *beckons over* INJURED MAN. *The other* DISCIPLES *don't notice.* JESUS *whispers to the* INJURED MAN *and he nods and lies down on the ground. The other* DISCIPLES *then all exit as if talking to one another, still rather smug. They walk right over* INJURED MAN. *Just as they are all about to disappear they suddenly stop and turn slowly, aware of the*

INJURED MAN. *They look at* JESUS. *He beckons them to help* INJURED MAN. *They point at themselves in disbelief.* JESUS *nods. They look to one another and then shamefacedly come to pick up* INJURED MAN. *They 'chair' him off.* JESUS *smiles and comes forward to the audience.)*

JESUS: Now you go and do the same!

(JESUS *pauses for count of three, and then exits.)*

* * *

IDEAS FOR A LINK-UP WITH 'PARABLE OF THE SOWER'

The actors form a line across the area, their backs to the audience. Starting from SR the actors turn, one after the other, and hold up a large letter on a card so that the whole line reads PARABLES. *Then from SL they turn upstage again. They turn to face the audience again in the same way, from SR, but this time the cards have been turned around and the line reads* THE SOWER. *They turn away. The person at the end, SL, goes down the line collecting the cards and he or she then stands DR to act as the first narrator for 'The Sower'. The rest of the group all have their heads lowered as if asleep and on 'Listen!' the heads all jerk upright and they turn one after another, and then the script continues as before.*

At the end after 'Then listen!' the actors turn upstage, one after the other in sequence with the first narrator going down the line giving out cards and joining the end of it. Then all turn as before, from SR, holding up cards, so that the line reads KINDNESS. *They all turn away and the person at the other end of the line, SR, moves down the line collecting up the cards. He or she moves DL to become the second narrator. The 'Good Samaritan' is then enacted and at the end all the actors re-form their line with their backs to the audience, with the second narrator going down the line giving out cards and joining the end of it, SR. Then all turn so that the line reads* FINISHED. *The actors turn away. Then they turn back, having changed the cards around, so that the line reads* GOD BLESS.

They all turn away and exit to either side.

N.B. Instead of card, cubes with letters on could be used. Instead of being collected they could be left US by actors during pieces.

Psalm 23

CHARACTERS: PSALMIST
Seven ACTORS

Notes:

1. A soft spotlight on PSALMIST *could enhance the effect, and suitable music could help create atmosphere. A flute can be most effective, capturing the different moods of rage and calm, menace and peace.*

2. The piece relies heavily on movement, but do not be put off by this! The movements are generally threatening—angular, expansive, with use of facial expressions. A good way into this is to just spend some moments on expressing the words 'darkness', 'despair', 'defeat', 'death', etc. in movement as they are called out. Try to then portray them in different ways of physical expression. Then hold body freezes for each word as it is called out. Do the same warm-up for the 'I want' phrases, and the 'no time' phrases.

3. The PSALMIST *must project a quality of peace in the midst of all that is going on around.*

SCENE: PSALMIST *stands or sits in the centre of the area. Behind him in a semi-circle are seven* ACTORS. *They could all be dressed in basic black. The* PSALMIST *is in ordinary clothes or black top and other coloured trousers or skirt. The* ACTORS *take up the chant 'I want', each one adding his voice to previous one. When the last one has joined in the chant, all stop. Each 'want' is then expressed with suitable emphasis and gesture.*

ACTOR 1: I want more money!
ACTOR 2: I want a new car!
ACTOR 3: I want some new clothes!
ACTOR 4: I want a new wife!
ACTOR 5: I want a sunshine holiday!

ACTOR 6: I want some expensive jewellery!

ACTOR 7: I want as much as I can get!

(Each ACTOR *adopts a frozen position, after chanting line, suitable to their line. At the end, the group again take up the chant 'I want'. When the last one has joined the others they all stop.)*

PSALMIST: The Lord is my shepherd, I shall not want.

*(*ACTORS *begin to chant 'no time' each one adding his or her voice in turn. When the last one has joined in the chant, all stop. All dart about the area in a terrible hurry. As they do so one or two words and phrases are heard.)*

ACTOR 1: Taxi!

ACTOR 2: Excuse me, could you tell me....

ACTOR 3: Sorry, can't stop.

ACTOR 4: Come on hurry along there!

ACTOR 5: Out of my way!

ACTOR 6: Is this the right way to....

ACTOR 7: I don't know!

(Everyone freezes in frenzied attitude.)

PSALMIST: He makes me lie down in green pastures. He leads me beside still waters. He restores my soul.

(Over this last sentence six ACTORS *move slowly and painfully into three parallel lines, behind* PSALMIST, *facing the audience. Each one places his left hand on the shoulder in front and hangs his head down. The odd one out moves slowly to the top of one of the lines, USC.)*

ACTOR 7: This is the way!

(He starts to walk down it slowly, but suddenly it changes as ACTORS *turn to the right and again put hands on shoulders of person next to them, making line run across stage left to right.)*

(More frantically.) No! This must be the way!

(As he slowly moves forwards ACTORS *move back again to form original lines.)*

(Very frantically.) No, no! *This* must be the way!

(They all freeze.)

PSALMIST: He leads me in paths of righteousness for his name's sake.

*(*ACTORS *slowly lower their arms to their sides, raise heads, and turn on* PSALMIST, *threateningly, while moving to a semi-*

circular shape behind him. They slowly raise their right arms and point at him. All whisper loudly 'death', then lunge towards him, right leg and right arm extended, crying 'death'. Each hand should be only fractionally away from PSALMIST. ACTORS *slowly encircle* PSALMIST *at different levels, menacing him. The actions represent the forces of evil all around, threatening the* PSALMIST. *Lots of body, arm, and hand movements here. Use of facial expression. It should be a slow build up of threat. As the* ACTORS *circle, certain words are whispered out at him. 'Darkness', 'despair', 'defeat', 'death', 'trapped', 'tortured', 'terror'. These also build with the movement until a climax of movement and word is reached. The* PSALMIST *throws up his arms and lets them fall slowly back to his sides.)*

PSALMIST: Even though I walk through the valley of the shadow of death, I fear no evil. For you are with me. Your rod and staff, they comfort me.

(As PSALMIST *says these words,* ACTORS *fall away into two parallel lines and he slowly walks forward between them as they still try to reach for him and menace him. At the end of the lines* PSALMIST *stops, his arms spread open.)*

You prepare a table before me in the presence of my enemies.

(The two lines link to form a semi-circle behind him and again at different levels they try to reach out for PSALMIST. *A lot of angular movement of body, arm and hand. The effect should be of being close enough to devour* PSALMIST, *but just failing.)*

You anoint my head with oil, my cup overflows.

*(*PSALMIST *looks up as he begins this sentence and raises his hands up as if holding a giant cup which then spills out refreshingly over his upturned face. The group desperately try to reach up for the cup, clawing upwards, despair more and more showing on their faces and in their movements.* PSALMIST *lowers his arms to his sides.* ACTORS *hold various positions of despair at various levels, around him.)*

Surely goodness and mercy will follow me all the days of my life.

(Each of the group then calls out one of the words used before against PSALMIST *but this time they are its prey, and as they say the word they hold an attitude appropriate to it.)*

ACTOR 1: Trapped!
ACTOR 2: Tortured!
ACTOR 3: Terror!
ACTOR 4: Darkness!
ACTOR 5: Despair!
ACTOR 6: Defeat!
ACTOR 7: Death!

(ACTORS *are like wax works as they hold their attitude.)*

PSALMIST: And I will dwell in the house of the Lord for ever.

(PSALMIST *raises his head and hands in adoration.)*

The Body

CHARACTERS: NARRATOR
Five ACTORS (or more)

Notes:

1. This piece is particularly recommended for use in a church context, perhaps when there is a sermon on 'the body of Christ'.

2. The unity movements at the beginning and end need to flow in unison—slowly and gracefully. Obviously the downstage 'line' of the triangle is not filled or the audience would not see. Where total unity is suggested, the downstage actors extend their free arms to each other.

3. Exaggerated movements are needed to express disharmony and disarray. The spoken lines by the body need to be crisp. The movements of caring for one another need to be genuine, and not sickly.

SCENE: NARRATOR *is at one side of the area. Upstage centre is a line of* ACTORS *facing the audience, one behind the other.*

NARRATOR: Christ is like a single body which has many parts.

(ACTOR *furthest DS moves DSR. Next* ACTOR *moves DSL. Rest move in turn alternately left and right. Each stands slightly towards SC. The lines aim towards USC. The* ACTOR *furthest US therefore does not move but forms the apex.* ACTORS *thus form two sides of a triangle, the apex USC.)*

It is still one body even though it is made up of different parts. In the same way, all of us, whether Jews or Gentiles, whether slaves or free *(On 'Jews', 'Gentiles', 'slaves' and 'free' either one or two* ACTORS, *depending on numbers, turn inwards to signify these areas.)* have been baptized *(All* ACTORS *slowly raise their arms vertically and then lower the arms with elbows bent, down through the body.)* into one body *(The arms come up behind and around in a horizontal position to encompass everybody.)* by the same Spirit, *(The arms are raised to a vertical position, palms open.)* and we have all been given the one Spirit to drink. *(The arms are lowered, with elbows bent, as the hands go down through the mouth and body and rest at the sides.)*

For the body itself is not made up of only one part *(The 'sides' of the triangle collapse leaving only the one figure upright.)* but of many parts. *(They all slowly rise again.)*

If the foot were to say

ACTOR 1: Because I am not a hand I don't belong to the body. *(He turns to face outside triangle.)*

NARRATOR: That would not keep it from being part of the body. *(*ACTOR 1, *surprised, turns in again.)* And if the ear were to say

ACTOR 2: Because I am not an eye I don't belong to the body. *(*ACTOR 2, *preferably from the other side of the triangle, turns to face outside triangle.)*

NARRATOR: That would not keep it from being a part of the body. *(*ACTOR 2, *surprised, turns in again.)*

If the whole body were just an eye *(All* ACTORS *hold a 'lookout' position with palm across the eyes, torsos bent forward.)* How could it hear? *(*ACTORS *look puzzled and shrug shoulders.)* And if it were only an ear *(*ACTORS *put palms against ears.)* how could it smell? *(*ACTORS *look puzzled again and shrug. They gather together in the centre, rather disconsolate.)*

As it is, however, *(they look up hopefully)* God put every different part in the body just as he wanted it to be.

*(*ACTORS *become happy and scurry about with tremendous zest until each one resumes former position in the triangle and contentedly 'settles' into it.)*

There would not be a body if it were all only one part. *(The 'sides' of the triangle collapse again.)* As it is there are many parts but one body. *(They all leap up excitedly, shake hands energetically with one another and return to their positions.)*
So then the eye cannot say to the hand

ACTOR 2: I don't need you! *(*ACTOR 2 *turns away sadly.)*

NARRATOR: Nor can the head say to the feet

ACTOR 4: I don't need you! *(*ACTOR 3 *becomes 'feet' and turns away sadly.)*

NARRATOR: On the contrary, we cannot do without the parts of the body that seem to be weaker. *(*ACTOR 1 *and* ACTOR 3 *turn in again, looking happy, and wag their fingers at* ACTOR 2 *and* ACTOR 4 *respectively.)*
And those parts that we think aren't worth very much *(Another* ACTOR *or two hang their heads down.)* are the ones which we treat with greater care.
*(*ACTORS *on either side comfort them, restoring them.)*
While the parts of the body which don't look very nice *(Another* ACTOR *or two hide their faces away.)* are treated with special modesty which the more beautiful parts do not need. *(*ACTORS *on either side gently reassure them.)*
God himself has put the body together *(All* ACTORS *raise their arms upwards.)* in such a way as to give greater honour to those parts that need it. *(All arms are lowered with elbows bent, and then brought around in a horizontal position to encompass everybody.)*
And so there is no division in the body, *(All arms are lowered and hands are joined.)* but all its different parts have the same concern for one another. *(Each pair embraces. Then they return to their position.)*
If one part of the body suffers *(One* ACTOR *half crumples as if hit in the stomach.)* all the other parts suffer with it. *(The other* ACTORS *crumple likewise. They then all return to their positions.)*
If one part is praised *(One* ACTOR *raises hands as in triumph.)* all the other parts share its happiness. *(Other* ACTORS *raise their arms towards* ACTOR *in acknowledgement. Then they all revert to neutral.)*
All of you are Christ's body *(*ACTORS' *arms are raised*

upwards slowly, palms open, heads lifted up. They kneel.) and each one is a part of it. *(The arms come down through the body, around and over each other's shoulders, so that the* ACTORS *are linked.)*

The Twentieth-Century Church?

CHARACTERS: NARRATOR
Six ACTORS (or more)

Notes:
1. The actors could all be in basic black. The figure of JESUS *could have black trousers and a different coloured top.*
2. This piece really needs linking to a talk in a church meeting, relevant as it is to Christians who think they're all right in their little religious enclaves, and to those who need to ask Jesus into their lives.

SCENE: *A line of* ACTORS *enter from SR and SL and stand across the area facing the people. Their heads are to one side as if asleep. They could be snoring.*

NARRATOR: *(on mike offstage or from lectern)* To the angel of the church in Laodicea. *(*ACTORS *suddenly wake and become alert.)* This is the message from the Amen, the faithful and true witness, who is the origin of all that God has created. I know what you have done. *(*ACTORS *look terribly proud and pleased with themselves. They polish halos, mark up a score, rub knuckles on chest, etc.)*
I know that you are neither cold *(*ACTORS *shiver exaggeratedly.)* nor hot. *(*ACTORS *wipe sweat off brows, pant exaggeratedly, even take off articles of clothing.)* How I wish you were either one *(exaggerated cold again)* or the other! *(exaggerated heat again)* But because you are lukewarm *(*ACTORS *start looking extremely offended, pointing at themselves in disbelief.)*

ACTORS: Lukewarm?!

NARRATOR: Neither hot *(exaggerated heat again)* nor cold *(exaggerated cold again)* I am going to spit you out of my mouth! *(On 'spit'* ACTORS *are propelled forward and land among the audience. They apologize profusely, back off, dust themselves down and resume their former line with great embarrassment.)*

You say, 'I am rich and well off.'

ACTORS: *(mumbling)* I am rich and well off!

NARRATOR: 'I have all I need.'

ACTORS: *(bolder)* I have all I need!

(ACTORS *then repeat these two phrases, each person taking one word, to be followed quickly by the next: 'I...am...rich... and...etc.' Try to get a rise and fall in pitch on each word. When the last person has said a word then* ACTORS *sing the phrases to the tune of 'Girls and boys come out to play', adding the word 'very' before 'well'. When the group have sung 'I am rich and very well off, I have all I ne-ed', twice, then they sing it again—this time making a 'roundel' of it, singing and weaving their way in and out of one another as on May day. The song is repeated several times, getting faster and faster. Eventually they collapse against one another, full of mirth.)*

NARRATOR: But you do not know how miserable and pitiful you are. (ACTORS *are propelled forward, each one getting thrown to the floor.)*

You are poor, (ACTORS *become crippled beggars begging for alms.)* naked *(They try to cover themselves.)* and blind *(They become blind. Their hands go to their faces. They feel and claw the air, stumbling, and groping.)* I advise you then to buy gold from me, pure gold, in order to be rich. *(A figure representing* JESUS *appears behind them upstage. He could appear before the word 'miserable'. The people grope their way towards him, begging.)*

Buy also white clothing to dress yourself and cover up your shameful nakedness. (ACTORS *'buy' clothing and mime putting on robes.)* Buy also some ointment to put on your eyes, so that you may see. *(They 'buy' ointment and put it on their eyes. They then show the wonder of new sight, and seeing* JESUS *they fall to their knees, heads to the ground, away from him.)*

I rebuke and punish all whom I love. Be in earnest then, and turn from your sins. *(*ACTORS *slowly lift their heads, and turn so that they are facing* JESUS. *They raise their arms to him in adoration.)* Listen!

*(*ACTORS *slowly rise. Four form a door. They are side by side centrestage, backs to audience. They are in two pairs, each pair with arms around the shoulders. The door will then open from the middle, DSC. The door is shut though to begin with. The other* ACTOR *stays in the area, DS while* JESUS *is behind the door, upstage.)*

I stand at the door and knock. *(The* ACTOR *in the area lifts his head, 'hearing'.)* If anyone hears my voice and opens the door *(The man comes to the door and opens it.* JESUS *stands in the doorway.)* I will come into his house and eat with him, and he will eat with me. *(*JESUS *enters and offers his hand or hands to the person. He takes them. Freeze.)*

*(*ACTORS *resume former line, as if asleep again.* JESUS *exits.)*

If you have ears, then listen to what the Spirit says to the churches!

(Very quietly, and as if still asleep, the group sing 'I am rich and very well off' once through. Freeze. ACTORS *exit SR and SL.)*

Faith Without Works

CHARACTERS: JAMES
Six ACTORS (or more)

Notes:
1. It is possible to do this more as a reading, with JAMES *doing the reading from the Bible.*
2. Lighting instructions (optional) are in brackets. There is no real problem with a lack of lights, apart from the 'judgement' section. After 'judges the man who has not been merciful' the ACTORS *hold a frozen tableau, with hands and arms raised shielding faces as if from*

dazzling light. After 'mercy triumphs over judgement' the pair DSL hold frozen tableau of arms and heads and hands raised in worship, accepted by the light. Pause. Freezes break. Pair leave area.

SCENE: JAMES *paces up and down. There is a table and chair stage right with a quill and paper on it. There is a spotlight on him.*

JAMES: *(to himself)* From James, a servant of God and of the Lord Jesus Christ. Greetings to all God's people scattered over the whole world. My friends...my friends... *(Stops, then hurries to his table. Writes and reads aloud.)* My friends, what good is it for a person to say, 'I have faith,' if their actions do not prove it? Can that faith save the person? Suppose there are brothers and sisters who need clothes and don't have enough to eat. What good is there in your saying to them, 'God bless you! Keep warm and eat well!' if you don't give them the necessities of life!

(Procession of ACTORS *enters upstage left, hands clasped in prayer. They chant or organ music is played. They form a semi-circle to James' left. Centre area is lit.)*

This is how it is with faith. If it is alone and has no actions with it then it is dead. *(Spotlight off.)*

*(*ACTORS *kneel, bow their heads, rise then go through a mime and word sequence as follows. The leader gives the cue for 'prayer'—hands in prayer saying the word all together. Then 'worship'—hands raised upwards, repeating the word at the same time. 'Bible study'—hands together as holding a book, repeating the word. 'Fellowship'—hands to sides, slightly outwards but not touching, repeating the word. Continue this pattern in a very monotonous tone and rhythm. A* PERSON *walks up the aisle. Looks at the group going through their ritual. Eventually tries to break in.)*

PERSON: I say... *(*ACTORS *stop speaking but continue actions.)* Well, don't let me stop you. You carry on. I'm new here you see. *(He tries to talk with several of the* ACTORS*, getting no response as they continue their actions.)*

Just moved in up the road. Very pleasant, isn't it? Have you been here long? Are you married? Any children? What's there to do for the kids then? Do you have a Sunday School? Of course you must have a Sunday

School. Young Wives, perhaps? She likes that. I'm sorry if I'm disturbing you. The door was open you see. I thought it would be all right if I came in. There was a board outside: 'Everyone welcome.' I mean it is a church, isn't it. Isn't it? Well why don't you talk to me? *(Grabs hold of one of them. They all speak again in conjunction with the actions, getting quicker and quicker.)*

What's wrong with me? I haven't got the plague, you know. Oh, go to hell!

(ACTORS *audibly gasp and fall into a huddle, faces hidden. They mutter 'language' and 'tut-tut', then fall silent.* PERSON *walks off in disgust SR.)*

JAMES: *(with spotlight on him)* So you see a person is put right with God by what they do and not because of faith alone. *(One* ACTOR *looks up, listening.)* For just as the body without the spirit is dead, so faith without actions is also dead. *(Spotlight off.)*

(ACTOR *stands up, looks at others. Touches one, trying to communicate what he's suddenly realized, but as each one is touched they spring up, look at* ACTOR *for an embarrassed second, then spin around and desperately try to find their formula again, silently.* ACTOR *left alone breaks down and rushes out of the group, head buried in hands downstage left. Hold in spotlight.* PERSON *re-enters and notices the* ACTOR *alone.)*

PERSON: You all right? What's up? What's the matter? Here, steady on. You live around here? (ACTOR *nods.)* Well come on then, I'll see you home. That's it. *(They freeze.)*

(ACTORS *are left still trying to find their order. They speak again. Slowly they all regain their formula and former positions, and as they do so, there is tremendous satisfaction, even life about their recital, then they become monotonous again. Finally end on 'prayer', with hands in prayer attitude, standing silent.)*

JAMES: *(in spotlight)* God will not show mercy when he judges the person who has not been merciful; but mercy triumphs over judgement. *(Spotlight off group after 'merciful'. Leave spot on James. There should be a spot on pair DSL, and with words 'mercy triumphs' they leave stage. Spotlight off.)* Do not speak against one another. Whoever speaks against his brother or sister or judges them, speaks against the law of God and judges it.

(Spot off. Spot on ACTORS *holding exactly the same position. They start up their ritual again, going through it twice without speaking to get into rhythm. Then on each phrase one* ACTOR *voices a thought. Everyone holds the attitude while this happens. Then the* ACTORS *move and speak the next phrase, holding the attitude while the next* ACTOR *voices a thought.* [*see below*].*)*

ACTOR 1: *(in attitude of prayer with the rest)* Fifty pence in the collection, and they live in that great big house!

ACTOR 2: ('worship') No wonder his wife looks unhappy. The way he drones on, it's a wonder she's still sane!

ACTOR 3: ('Bible study') Just 'cos she's done the flowers, she thinks it's a passport to heaven!

ACTOR 4: ('Fellowship') If they sit in my pew one more time, I'll let their tyres down!

(With more people this can be continued. Having said a thought each the ACTORS *then voice their thoughts together still going through the actions and looking straight ahead, poker-faced. They rise to a pitch.)*

JAMES: *(with spotlight on him, breaking in)* God is the only law-giver and judge. *(They stop and look around.)* He alone can both save and destroy. Who do you think you are to judge your fellow man?

ACTORS: *(angrily)* Who does he think he is? How dare he? I never criticize anyone. The man's crazy! etc.

(Organ music gradually increases in volume and people drift out, still criticizing and grumbling. They may chant as they exit. Organ or chanting fades, as do the lights.)

JAMES: O my friends...my friends....

We Shall Overcome...

CHARACTERS: VOICES 1–5

Notes:
1. The group sculpture at the beginning and end should have VOICE *3 in the form of Jesus on the cross. The others take up various positions with regard to this e.g. one looking at him puzzled, another crouching away, another with his back to* VOICE *3, another kneeling with arms raised.*
2. The chorus lines 'We shall overcome' could be played at the beginning, increasing in volume, when group sculpture is set. Similarly, at the end, to fade out.
3. A podium or rostra block could be used for VOICE *3 for the sculptures and for the temptation episode. It is also very effective if a large crown of thorns is hung down, above the acting area, interlaced with red ribbon or paper.* VOICE *3 is then able at various points to stand beneath it.*
4. VOICE *3 should be strong but quiet, although in the temptation episode, the quietness gives way to a genuine struggle. This episode must give the impression of Jesus' struggles within himself and not exterior forces. Therefore in this episode the other* VOICES *must largely be from within the still shape form. Statements made by* VOICE *3 must be completely genuine.*
5. This piece works very well at Lent, and can be followed by a time of meditation and/or prayer, perhaps led by following certain themes which emerge from the piece.

It can also be linked to a larger programme, starting with 'Beast of a different burden' by Faith Whitehill, and 'Let's be devils' by Nevil Malin, published by S. French.

SCENE: ACTORS *enter one by one, in black, and form a sculpture—each waiting until previous* ACTOR *is in position before entering. The sculpture is formed on the theme of attitudes to the cross. It is important that three levels are used—high, medium and low, and that* VOICE *3 takes up a position upstage centre so that the others can later form a triangle from him.* VOICES *2 and 4 ought to be women. The opening lines are spoken from the freeze.*

VOICE 1: We shall overcome...
VOICE 5: Some day.
VOICE 2: We shall overcome...
VOICE 4: Some day.
VOICE 3: We shall overcome...
VOICES 1, 2, 4 & 5: Some day!
VOICE 3: Why can't we overcome today

(On their next lines VOICE *1 and* VOICE *2 break freeze and form one side of the triangle from* VOICE *3, and* VOICE *4 and* VOICE *5 form up the other side.* VOICE *1 is DL and* VOICE *5 is DR.* VOICE *3 stands on podium, but relaxes.)*

VOICE 1: Impossible!
VOICE 5: Out of the question!
VOICE 2: It's just not on!
VOICE 4: It's not that easy!
VOICE 3: But why not? *(The others turn their heads to* VOICE *3.)*
VOICES 1, 2, 4 & 5: Why not?
VOICE 3: Yes! Yes! Why not? *(They turn away again.* VOICE *3 sits on podium.)*
VOICES 1, 2, 4 & 5: Because we're human!
VOICE 2: The mark of Adam.
VOICE 3: The mark of Eve!
VOICE 4: The mark of Adam!
VOICE 1: The mark of Eve!

(The following lines are spat across at each other.)

VOICES 2 & 4: Adam!
VOICES 1 & 5: Eve!
VOICES 2 & 4: Adam!
VOICES 1 & 5: Eve!
VOICES 2 & 4: Adam!
VOICES 1 & 5: Eve!
VOICES 2 & 4: Adam!
VOICES 1 & 5: Eve!

VOICE 3: Stop it!

(The responses are forced and exaggerated)

VOICE 2: Sorry!

VOICE 5: My fault!

VOICE 4: Forgive me?

VOICE 1: I was to blame!

(Pause.)

VOICE 2: Yuk!

VOICE 5: Pardon?

VOICE 4: Yuk!

VOICE 1: What do you mean?

(Pause. Then they exchange insults.)

VOICE 2: Creep!

VOICE 5: Snake!

VOICE 4: Animal!

VOICE 1: Vegetable!

(Pause.)

VOICE 2: That's cruel!

VOICE 5: Well you started this!

VOICE 4: No we didn't!

VOICE 1: Yes you did!

VOICE 3: Stop it! Stop it! Why is it so much easier to present the problems than to solve them?

VOICE 2: Because it's easier

VOICE 5: Playing the baddy! *(Vocal intonation and stance of cowboy or devil with horns.)*

VOICE 4: Than playing

VOICE 1: The goody! *(Vocal intonation and stance of angel with halo.)*

VOICE 3: So what are we going to do?

VOICE 1: Not a lot.

VOICE 5: They're bored.

VOICE 2: And I'm bored.

VOICE 4: So let's go home! *(All moving.)*

VOICE 3: Be positive! Suggest something!

(Pause. VOICES *1, 2, 4 & 5 sigh and resume positions. They are irritated.)*

VOICE 1: There are so many problems

VOICE 5: Because there are so many people.

VOICE 2: So how can there be one answer
VOICE 4: To everybody's problem.
VOICE 3: But there is!
VOICES 1, 2, 4 & 5: Pardon? *(Turning upstage.)*
VOICE 3: There is.

(The others turn back with deep sighs. Then they somewhat shyly each take a certain section of the audience—easiest if semi-circular shape—and address the next few remarks to them, moving out of their triangle as they speak.)

VOICE 1: I have a constant worry over money.
VOICE 5: I have a constant worry over health.
VOICE 2: I worry about my job and the future.
VOICE 4: I worry about my exams. Success or failure?

(Pause.)

VOICE 1: I have a problem with my parents. There's so little communication. We're just growing apart.

VOICE 5: I have a problem in expressing myself. It's all bottled up inside. I feel frustrated and angry.

VOICE 2: My problem's simple. I feel that I'm wasting my life. Missing out. Failing.

VOICE 4: My problem is constant worry. Everything looms large. Small incidents are big problems.

VOICES 1 & 5: *(turning to each other)* So how can there be one answer

VOICES 2 & 4: *(turning to each other)* To all these problems?

VOICES 1, 2, 4 & 5: *(turning to* VOICE *3. They are growing irritable.)* And we are just four out of millions.

VOICE 1: And we've only mentioned
VOICE 5: A few of our worries,
VOICE 2: A few of our problems.
VOICE 4: Only a few.

(Pause.)

VOICE 1: What about the constant everyday niggles and nuisances

VOICE 5: Which crowd our lives and take up so much time?
VOICE 2: Oh yes! They're so often silly and stupid
VOICE 4: But at the time they're real problems.

(Pause. VOICE *5 and* VOICE *2 come in to the area. Freeze.* VOICE *2 has back to* VOICE *5. They then break the freeze.)*

VOICE 5: Have you seen my keys?
VOICE 2: What?
VOICE 5: *(growing more exasperated)* Have you seen my keys?
VOICE 2: No.
VOICE 5: Well they must be somewhere! And I'm late!
VOICE 2: I haven't got them!
VOICE 5: You could at least help me look for them!
VOICE 2: They're probably in your other jacket.
VOICE 5: They're not. I've looked. Are you sure you haven't had them?
VOICE 2: Of course I haven't had them.
VOICE 5: Well somebody's had them! They can't have just disappeared.
VOICE 2: Oh stop shouting!
VOICE 5: I'm late! *(Freeze. Centre of area. Then* VOICES *1 & 4 take up positions in area. Freeze. Break freeze to start.)*

(Pause.)

VOICE 1: Forty-five pounds!
VOICE 4: How much?
VOICE 1: Forty-five pounds! That's ridiculous. That's twice as much as last quarter.
VOICE 4: There must be some mistake. It can't have just doubled.
VOICE 1: That's all we need. More than a hundred pounds overdrawn and now this.
VOICE 4: We haven't paid the telephone bill yet either.
VOICE 1: Oh heck! It's just not fair. We never seem to get straight. What do we do now?
VOICE 4: Well, we'll just have to live off the Family Allowance and not go to the bank for a month.
VOICE 1: Oh yeah! And what do we do about the bills?
VOICE 4: I don't know. I suppose we could query it.
VOICE 1: It just goes on, and on, and on. I'm fed up with it!

(Freeze. Both pause then break freeze on their next lines.)

VOICE 2: Two incidents
VOICE 5: From daily life
VOICE 1: In the everyday story
VOICE 4: Of ordinary folk.

(Pause. The next section builds in pace and tempo as the actors

move about the area, firing the comments at the audience and each other.)

VOICE 1: Not to mention
VOICE 5: The car tax
VOICE 2: Running out
VOICE 4: And the MOT
VOICE 1: Add to that
VOICE 4: The broken drainpipe,
VOICE 5: The loose tiles,
VOICE 2: The rising damp
VOICE 4: And the rising mortgage.

(All VOICES *stop for a moment before moving into the next phase of complaints aimed at each other and the audience. Build in tempo.)*

VOICE 1: Then there's family squabbles:
VOICE 5: Which TV channel?
VOICE 2: Why shouldn't I?
VOICE 4: Why should you?
VOICE 1: Throw in the job.
VOICE 5: Dissatisfaction
VOICE 2: With the old man
VOICE 4: And his snoring.
VOICE 1: And the wife,
VOICE 5: With her nagging.
VOICE 2: And the kitchen sink
VOICE 4: With the garden fence
VOICES 1 & 2: And you've got yourself
VOICES 4 & 5: A daily dose of problems! *(Worn out!)*
VOICE 3: Not forgetting the neighbours!

*(*VOICES *1, 2, 4 & 5 turn heads inwards and smile.* VOICES *1 & 2 form a couple on one side of the garden fence and* VOICES *4 & 5 form a couple on the other side. Freeze. Then break freeze. The opening exchanges are sugary sweet and drawn out. Little waves etc!)*

VOICES 1 & 2: Hello there!
VOICES 4 & 5: Hello!
VOICES 1 & 2: Lovely day!
VOICES 4 & 5: Yes. Lovely.

(Pause. They all turn back again. Whisper to each other.)

VOICE 1: Why can't they fix that fence?
VOICE 2: And keep that blasted dog quiet at night!
VOICE 4: I do wish they'd keep their children under control!
VOICE 5: And not keep parking outside our house!

(Pause. They all turn heads inwards and smile. Freeze. Unfreeze.)

VOICES 1 & 2: Hello there!
VOICES 4 & 5: Hello!
VOICES 1 & 2: Lovely day!
VOICES 4 & 5: Yes. Lovely. *(Freeze.)*

(Pause. They all turn back again. They address their remarks to their part of the audience, moving to them.)

VOICE 1: And all we've done
VOICE 5: Is to scratch the surface of the problems
VOICE 2: Which beset us all
VOICE 4: From the cradle to the grave.
VOICE 1: And each problem
VOICE 5: Needs a different answer,
VOICE 2: Because behind each problem
VOICE 4: Lies a different person.
VOICES 1 & 5: *(turning to face* VOICE *3)* So how can there be one answer
VOICES 2 & 4: *(turning to face* VOICE *3)* To everybody's problem?
VOICE 3: Because everybody's problem is the same.

(Pause. Their responses are sarcastic, drawing in the audience onto their side.)

VOICE 1: As simple as that!
VOICE 5: Obviously!
VOICE 2: No doubt about it!
VOICE 4: It's cut and dried!

(They slowly turn heads to look at VOICE *3.)*

VOICES 1, 2, 4 & 5: What's the common problem then? *(This is said as if talking to a child.)*
VOICE 3: Human nature.

*(*VOICE *3 rises and slowly moves into area. They all turn back on their reply. Use of audience again.)*

VOICES 1, 2, 4 & 5: *(emphatically)* Yuk!
VOICE 3: Self.

VOICE 1: Too easy!
VOICE 3: Putting self first and others second.
VOICE 5: Too simple!
VOICE 3: Putting self instead of God at the centre of life.
VOICE 2: Too religious!
VOICE 3: Man's nature is biased towards self-interest.
VOICE 4: Too emphatic!

(Pause. They slowly turn heads to look at VOICE *3.)*

VOICES 1, 2, 4 & 5: What's the common answer then? *(Childish again.)*

VOICE 3: A right relationship with God.

(They all turn back on their reply. Shake heads at audience.)

VOICES 1, 2, 4 & 5: *(even more emphatically)* Yuk!
VOICE 3: God wants a relationship with everyone day by day.
VOICE 1: Too busy!
VOICE 3: He wants total honesty.
VOICE 5: Too frightening!
VOICE 3: Absolute commitment.
VOICE 2: Too permanent!
VOICE 3: And a growing awareness that we can do nothing without him.
VOICE 4: Too repressive!

(Pause. They slowly turn heads to look at VOICE *3.)*

VOICES 1, 2, 4 & 5: Words! It's all words! Where's the proof?
VOICE 3: Jesus.

(They all turn back on their reply. Shake heads.)

VOICES 1, 2, 4 & 5: *(more emphatic still)* Yuk!
VOICE 3: Jesus is God's answer to man's problems.
VOICE 1: Trite!
VOICE 3: Jesus is man's only salvation.
VOICE 5: Evangelitudes!
VOICE 3: Without Jesus there can be no overcoming.
VOICE 2: Narrow minded!
VOICE 3: Only Jesus' love can deal with man's human nature.
VOICE 4: Pulpitudes!

(Pause. They then in turn move up to VOICE *3 venting their*

frustration.)

VOICE 1: Me! What about me! Don't I matter?

VOICE 4: My problems! What about my pathetic, insignificant little problems which drag me down and sap my life?

VOICE 5: I'm me! I'm not just any person. Hey! You're talking to me!

VOICE 2: Disappointed, frustrated, embittered! That's me. Go bury your religious platitudes!

VOICES 1, 2, 4 & 5: Can't you see?

(They all turn back. Their next remarks are to 'their' part of the audience.)

VOICE 1: How can one man take up everybody's problems

VOICE 2: And still treat each person as unique and special?

VOICE 5: And how can one man meet everybody's needs

VOICE 4: Totally?

VOICE 3: Because he created you. Because he lived for you. Because he died for you.

(The next remarks are said with growing frustration to 'their' part of the audience.)

VOICE 1: But he was so good!

VOICE 5: So perfect!

VOICE 2: So right!

VOICE 4: So transparent!

VOICES 1, 2, 4 & 5: When did he really struggle?

VOICE 3: All his life.

VOICES 1, 2, 4 & 5: *(turning to* VOICE *3)* But when? when?

VOICE 1: *(sinking to the ground)* When did he ever nearly fail?

VOICE 5: *(similarly)* When did he ever feel like giving up?

VOICE 2: *(similarly)* When did temptation ever really worry him?

VOICE 4: *(similarly)* When did he ever really identify with me?

(Pause. Lighting change. Spot on VOICE *3. Other area dim. Other* VOICES *take on the tone of tempter. Physically they are all curled up in rock shapes. The* VOICES *are insistent & insidious, and* VOICE *3 takes up a lot of their lines.)*

VOICE 1: If you are the Son of God

VOICE 3: You are my beloved Son.

VOICE 5: If you are the Son of God
VOICE 3: You are my beloved Son.
VOICE 2: If you are the Son of God
VOICE 3: You are my beloved Son.
VOICE 4: If you are the Son of God
VOICE 1: If!
VOICE 5: If!
VOICE 2: If!
VOICE 4: If!
VOICES 1, 2, 4 & 5: If, if, if, if!
VOICE 3: If?
VOICE 1: Command these stones to be loaves of bread.
VOICE 3: Loaves of bread!
VOICE 5: Go on! You're hungry! So very hungry! Hungry!
VOICE 3: Hungry! *(He stoops.)*
VOICE 2: Just turn them to bread! What's wrong with that? You're hungry! And it's so very easy!
VOICE 3: Easy! What's wrong with that? I'm hungry.
VOICE 4: What are you waiting for? Just command! Just command! Just command!
VOICE 3: Command! Stones to bread...
VOICES 1, 2, 4, 5 & 3: Stones to bread! Stones to bread! Stones to bread! Stones to bread!
VOICE 3: No! *(Rises. Pause.)*
VOICE 1: You can't do it! You can't do it!
VOICE 5: Son of God? Are you...are you? Then prove yourself.
VOICE 2: Where's your power, Jesus? Are you the Christ? You've failed! You've failed before you've begun.
VOICE 3: Failed! Are you the Christ?
VOICE 1: What's the point of going on
VOICE 5: If you can't even do this?
VOICE 3: What's the point?
VOICE 2: Exactly! There is no point!
VOICE 4: It's useless! Quite useless! Just like you!
VOICES 1, 2, 4, 5 & 3: Useless, useless, useless, useless, useless, useless, useless!

(On the last word VOICE *3 picks up a 'stone' and hurls it.)*

VOICE 3: No! Man shall not live by bread alone, but by the

word of God. Remember the people of Israel? How God supplied their need in the wilderness? Must I supply my own in case he fails me? Trust him. Trust in his sure promise that he will provide. Am I not his Son?

VOICE 1: *(Suddenly rising and spinning around to face* VOICE *3.)* If you are the Son of God!

VOICE 5: *(rising and spinning)* If!

VOICE 2: *(rising and spinning)* If!

VOICE 4: *(rising and spinning)* If!

VOICE 3: If? *(*VOICES *1, 2, 4 & 5 carry* VOICE *3 onto podium, then return to their places.)*

VOICE 1: *(spinning slowly back and down again)* Throw yourself down!

VOICE 5: *(similarly)* Down!

VOICE 2: *(similarly)* Down!

VOICE 4: *(similarly)* Down!

VOICE 1: For it is written!

VOICE 5: Written!

VOICE 2: Written

VOICE 4: Written!

VOICE 3: It is written!

VOICE 1: He will give his angels charge of you!

VOICE 3: Angels charge of you!

VOICES 1 & 2: *(echoing)* Angels charge of you...charge of you...charge of you...

VOICE 5: And on their hands they will bear you up!

VOICE 3: Bear you up!

VOICES 4 & 5: *(echoing)* Bear you up...bear you up... bear you up!

VOICE 3: Lest you should strike your foot against a stone! It is written. It is written.

VOICE 2: Miracle!

VOICE 4: Miracle!

VOICE 1: Miracle!

VOICE 5: Miracle!

VOICE 3: Miracle!

VOICE 2: Prove you are the Messiah! It's so easy!

VOICE 1: Give them a sign of your divinity! Just a sign!

VOICE 4: It is written, remember! God will provide.

VOICE 5: If you are the Son of God! You must prove it! You must!

VOICE 3: Must prove it! It is written. A miracle. It would be so easy!

VOICES 1, 2, 4 & 5: Prove it, prove it, prove it!

*(*VOICE *3 sways forward on their repeats.)*

VOICE 3: No! For it is also written, 'You shall not put the Lord your God to the test.' It is written, 'You shall not!' *(Pause.)*

VOICE 2: So much you could do!

VOICE 4: So much you could gain!

VOICE 1: So much you could enjoy!

VOICE 5: You shall not!

VOICE 3: You shall not!

VOICE 2: With your power what couldn't you do?

VOICE 4: Untold wealth and luxury.

VOICE 1: All of this and more would be yours to rule. Just yours!

VOICE 5: *(sulkily)* But you shall not!

VOICE 3: You shall not? *(Comes down from podium US then hurries into the area and looks out.)*

VOICE 2: You could be the world's greatest hero!

VOICE 4: You could have such glory!

VOICE 1: You could be King of kings—now!

VOICE 5: All you have to do...

VOICES 1, 2, 4 & 5: Is worship me!

VOICE 3: Worship?

VOICE 1: Think. Don't be hasty...all of this...now ...for all your life....

VOICE 2: *(sensuously)* Just for a moment's worship... that's all!

VOICE 5: Think of what you'll miss—all the power, all the wealth, all the glory....

VOICE 4: *(sensuously)* Just for a moment's worship....

VOICES 2 & 4: *(sensuously)* Worship...worship...worship....

VOICE 3: No! No! Get behind me Satan! For it is written in the Scriptures: 'You shall worship the Lord your God, and serve only him.' Fear God, worship God, be faithful to God. Alone. It is written.

*(*VOICE *3 has sunk to his knees by the end. The others slowly rise together.)*

VOICE 1: That's the difference

VOICE 2: Between him and me.

VOICE 4: He had such strength of character,

VOICE 5: Such use of the word of God.

VOICE 3: He has promised you his strength.

VOICE 1: But I fail!

VOICE 3: He has promised never to give you up!

VOICE 2: But I feel so alone!

VOICE 3: He has promised you victory over self!

VOICE 5: But I live with defeat!

VOICE 3: To those who overcome he has promised the victory. *(Each in turn then comes to* VOICE *3 with their reaction.)*

VOICE 1: *(angrily)* And where do you find the overcomers in the church? It's filled with spiritual cripples and paralytics and neurotics!

VOICE 3: He never promised it would be easy. Too many make that mistake. There is a cross for everyone who comes to Christ. It must be so.

VOICE 4: Why? Why must it be so? Why can't we live in love and harmony? Why must there be this striving?

VOICE 3: Because man's greatest problem is himself. Self must be constantly brought under the sway of Christ. And this is hard. This is the daily battle.

VOICE 5: But the daily battle for most of us is the current problem—not the victory over self. Your advice is good. It has been all along. But we won't change. Oh yes, we'll try! But we won't change. Can't you see that? *(Angrily and in despair.)* We won't change! *(Hangs head.)*

VOICE 2: He's right! That's the problem. Even knowing the answer we still fail. And try as we may, we know we'll fail. So what's the point? Whether we come to Christ or keep away, what difference does it make? Christ, where are you? *(Sinks to the ground.)*

(Slowly VOICE *1 goes over to* VOICE *5 and* VOICE *4 goes over to* VOICE *2.)*

VOICE 3: That's the difference Christ makes! When you

cry to him in honest need he will answer. His answer may not be what you expect but he will answer, and it will be for your good. And perhaps in being God's remedy for another's problem, you cure your own. *(The pairs look at one another.)* That's why God wants you to share and care.

VOICE 1: And you shall love your neighbour

VOICE 5: As yourself. *(They reach towards one another and are close to touching.)*

VOICE 4: *(helping* VOICE *2 up)* And you shall love your neighbour

VOICE 2: As yourself. *(They also reach towards one another and are close to touching.)*

(Both pairs are about to touch. Then suddenly they break away, each taking up an isolated position in the area.)

VOICE 1: It's too hard!

VOICE 2: *(echoing)* Too hard!

VOICE 4: *(echoing)* Too hard!

VOICE 5: *(echoing)* Too hard!

VOICE 3: 'And God said...' and it was done! (VOICES *1, 2, 4 & 5 move hurriedly around, hands on ears, interspersing* VOICE *3 lines with 'Too hard', in unison.)* 'And the word became flesh and dwelt among us.' 'If you love me, obey my commandments.' It is written...it is written ...it is written. You cannot hope to grow and overcome if you do not live by the word of God.

VOICES 1, 2, 4 & 5: Why? *(They stop suddenly.)*

VOICE 1: Why can't we just try our best and leave it at that?

VOICE 5: Why can't we just win a little, lose a little? That's more our level of living.

VOICE 2: Why get so serious? I know you're trying to help but it's all too much for us.

VOICE 4: Why all this emphasis on the word of God? Why?

VOICE 3: Because the devil will attack you at your weakest points. And they will become your greatest problems. If you have no armour to defend them you will be as good as dead, and your life will be wasted.

VOICES 1, 2, 4 & 5: *(scornfully)* the devil! *(They turn back to their part of the audience.)*

VOICE 3: Make no mistake. If Christ battled with Satan for survival, then so must you. For it is written, and will you call God a liar? But don't be afraid, for it is also written that Christ has overcome the devil, and his victory is your victory if you look to him and live out his word.

VOICE 1: *(Suddenly spinning around to face* VOICE *3, as do the others.)* Tell us honestly!

VOICE 2: Without hesitation!

VOICE 4: Will living by God's word

VOICE 5: Make our problems disappear?

VOICE 3: No.

VOICE 1: *(turning back sharply as do the others)* Exactly!

VOICE 2: At least he's honest!

VOICE 4: So much for Christ and the word then!

VOICE 5: So much for sermonizing!

(Pause.)

VOICE 3: Living by God's word may not make your problems disappear, but it will help you to overcome them.

(Each in turn addresses 'their' part of the audience with sarcasm.)

VOICE 1: I'm terribly sorry

VOICE 2: I can't pay the phone bill!

VOICE 4: But I'm living by God's word

VOICE 5: So please overlook it!

VOICE 1: *(sarcasm gives way to anger)* And this is just trivial

VOICE 2: Compared to some of the problems

VOICE 4: We have to face

VOICE 5: Day by day.

VOICES 1, 2, 4 & 5: This is the world we live in! *(They turn on* VOICE *3.)*

VOICE 3: 'I do not ask you to take them out of the world, but I do ask you to keep them safe from the Evil One. Just as I do not belong to the world they do not belong to the world. Dedicate them to yourself by means of the truth. Your word is truth. Don't be afraid. I have overcome the world.'

VOICES 1, 2, 4 & 5: But how do we

VOICES 1 & 5: Overcome

VOICES 2 & 4: Ourselves?

VOICE 3: By allowing God's Spirit to work in you, as you spend time with him day by day. The more you take in from God *(VOICES 1 & 4 slowly look up and reach up as if receiving.)* the more you can give out to others. *(VOICES 1 & 4 turn towards their partners and reach out to them. VOICES 2 & 5 turn inwards to face them.)* The greater your love for God, the greater will be your love for man. *(VOICES 1 & 4 move towards their partners.)* Whether you succeed *(VOICES 1 & 4 touch their partners.)* or fail *(VOICES 2 & 5 turn sharply away from partners.)* let your heart always be fixed on God *(VOICES 1 & 4 reach up.)* On Christ in you *(VOICES 1 & 4 reach out into the cross position, then draw the arms and hands into the chest.)* On the knowledge of his word *(VOICES 1 & 4 hold out their hands as if the Bible.)*

Then, be assured, you will overcome. *(They each resume their positions.)* But the choice must be yours. God's way or man's way. Which do you really want?

(The following remarks are made meditatively, showing different reactions, shared with different sections of the audience.)

VOICE 1: Christ wants me to live one day at a time, with him.

VOICE 5: But I want to be in charge. I want to plan my life.

VOICE 4: Christ wants me to put other people first.

VOICE 2: But I've got so much I want to do.

VOICE 1: Christ wants me to store up riches in heaven.

VOICE 5: I want to store up riches in the bank.

VOICE 4: Christ wants me to stand by his word, whatever the cost.

VOICE 2: I want to be popular, even if it means my standards slip a bit.

VOICE 1: Christ wants me to love all men, to be concerned.

VOICE 5: I don't want to get that involved. I can't even love half my relatives.

VOICE 4: Christ wants me to take up his cross and follow him.

VOICE 2: I'd rather do the best I can and leave it at that.

VOICE 1: *(with hope)* We shall overcome

VOICE 4: *(with hope)* Today!

VOICE 5: *(mockingly)* We shall overcome

VOICE 2: *(mockingly)* Some day!

*(*VOICE *3 has got up onto podium and assumed the cross shape, head bowed, arms extended, as he had in the beginning group sculpture.)*

VOICE 1: The trouble is, can I really live like that? I mean you've got to be practical.

VOICE 5: No one's ever lived like that.

VOICE 4: I suppose Jesus did.

VOICE 2: But look what happened to him. *(They turn and look at* VOICE *3. Over their last few comments they move back slowly towards their first positions in the group sculpture.)*

VOICE 1: So we're back where we started!

VOICE 5: No better off!

VOICE 4: Wiser though.

VOICE 2: But no better off!

VOICE 1: There's just a nagging doubt

VOICE 5: Going round in my mind

VOICE 4: That he could well be right!

VOICE 2: Uncomfortable, isn't it?

(They all hold their positions frozen. Light cut. Song of 'We shall overcome' could be played out here as lights fade. VOICES *then exit in the order in which they formed up sculpture, each waiting until the previous one has left the area.)*

Creation

CHARACTERS: NARRATOR
SIX ACTORS (or more)

Notes:

1. BENJY *must look very colourful and a trifle silly. The* ACTORS *ought to be in a basic colour, over which props and costumes are added.*

2. It is helpful if there is some kind of screen at the back of the area from which the ACTORS *appear.*

3. BENJY *and* ACTORS *mime throughout. The audience must see his ideas turn to frustration.*

4. The whole piece should be exhausting! Keep it bouncy.
5. The props needed should not have to be expensive. Placards (white card) can be used on both sides, and inscribed in thick felt tip pen. The paper that is thrown in is everyone's old newspapers, computer printouts, etc. in black sacks. This can be collected up later, especially if the area has some kind of stagecloth on the floor. The outsize pen can be made out of a large cardboard roll. Packing, to make a point, can fill in one end. Paper can be stuck around the roll and a felt tip used to draw lines on it, and the letters HB, etc. The coffee jar can again be made out of an outsize cardboard container, lined with paper and then drawn on. The graphics on props will hopefully be done by a member of the group, or someone interested in their work. The outsize bag of peanuts is made by creating a large bag out of heavy duty paper and drawing graphics on it. The large mug is made out of card, the law placards can be stapled onto wooden struts.

Most of the props therefore can be made out of card, and somebody keen on graphics will have fun.
6. The piece works well outside as well as inside. Beware of windy days with all the paper though!
7. This piece is useful in a Family Service or Youth Service, followed up later by a talk on creation.

SCENE: NARRATOR *enters, going to DSR to lectern or stand, and opens a big book. He or she could be offstage though with microphone.*

NARRATOR: In the beginning.... *(This is said in a very measured way. Suddenly the mood becomes bouncy.)* Benjy Bunting thought he had a good chance.

*(*BENJY *is chaired in by* ACTORS *to chorus of 'He's a jolly good fellow'. He is stood on a table centrestage.* ACTORS *stand around, cheering and clapping.)*

Well...he was an optimist! And nobody had really thought about it in this way before. You see, Benjy wanted to create a perfect world. *(*ACTORS *all mime a perfect round world.)* But in order to do this, somebody had to sit down and draw out plans, and write out certain guidelines. *(*ACTORS *all whisper to each other, pointing to* BENJY. *He has been preening himself throughout.)* And Benjy of course was the right person. *(*ACTORS *shout 'hurray'.)* Well it stood to reason. *(*ACTORS *nod.)* Benjy was...well, perfect himself!

*(*ACTORS *cheer.* BENJY *beams.* ACTORS *exit.)*

So Benjy set to work. *(*BENJY *jumps down and exits.)* First of all, *(*ACTOR *brings in placard with 'DAY 1' on it. Exit.)* he went down to the local stationers to buy himself enough paper, and pencils to last a week.

*(*ACTORS *enter from upstage. One carries a stack of paper, another an outsize pencil or pen. They put them on the table. Following them, other* ACTORS *bring placards. They line up in front of the table and one by one hold up placards to read '7 DAYS'. Last* ACTOR *holds up '?')*

Well, it was all the time he could afford. *(*ACTORS *exit as* BENJY *enters jauntily. Checks table.)* Then he went to the grocers to buy enough food, especially things to keep him alert... *(*ACTOR *appears upstage as grocer with apron and boater.)* like coffee *(hands* BENJY *outsize coffee jar)* and peanuts *(hands* BENJY *outsize packet of peanuts.)*

'Going on a diet, Mr Bunting?' said Sam, the grocer, pleased with his little joke. 'No', replied Benjy cheerfully, 'I'm creating a perfect world!' And off he went leaving Sam slightly worried as to whether it was he or Benjy who was completely mad.

*(*BENJY *exits.* SAM *scratches head and exits.)*

Benjy, on the other hand, had never felt better.

*(*ACTORS *enter from upstage doing keep-fit exercises one behind another around the area and exit.* BENJY *is the last in line.)*

He hurried home, bolted the door, *(this* BENJY *does)* and made himself a large mug of coffee. *(Goes SR to be handed an outsize mug. Takes it to desk.)* Then along with his peanuts *(peanut bag is thrown in)* he sat down *(he sits)* and started his work. First, he thought he'd draw plans. So he scribbled and drew, and drew, all that day.

*(*ACTORS *throw in paper from large sacks behind* BENJY, *as he scribbles and then scrumples up ideas and throws them on the floor.)*

By the end of it he hadn't got much to show, but no matter, he had a vague idea. *(*BENJY *scratches his head, looks at drawings in a puzzled way, and up at audience, holding expression.)* Benjy didn't sleep at all well that night....

(As BENJY *falls asleep at desk, two or three* ACTORS *appear as*

'ghosts', with sheets over heads, tormenting him. They exit with mug and peanuts.)

But in the morning, (ACTOR *enters with placard 'DAY 2'. Exits.* BENJY *awakes.)* he felt cheerful enough again, (BENJY *yawns, stretches, does a quick warm up, sits and smiles.)* and armed with more coffee, (ACTORS *throw in coffee jar and mug which he catches.)* and more peanuts, *(Peanut packet is thrown in.)* he set to work.

He drew up lists of what sort of people there ought to be, (BENJY *starts writing furiously. From SR an* ACTOR *appears with bowler and briefcase. From SL an* ACTOR *appears with flat cap and shovel.)* what they should do, (ACTORS *point to props.)* and where they should live. (BOWLER PERSON *depicts large house,* FLAT CAPPED PERSON *depicts small house.)* But somehow it all took longer, (ACTORS *try to cross stage to other side, but they keep to the same line each time as they try to pass each other, and frustrated they return to their places and exit, looking peeved.)* and used up more paper than he'd ever realized he would (ACTORS *throw in sacks of paper from upstage.)* By the time he was on his tenth mug of coffee, (BENJY *holds up mug as* ACTOR *appears with placard '10' on it, then exits.)* he was getting a little fed up. (ACTORS *enter with placards. They form a line behind* BENJY *and hold up placards together to read: 'FED UP'. They exit.)*

He looked around and was alarmed to see a large amount of paper building up around him. (ACTORS *throw in more paper.)* 'Order!' thought Benjy. 'We must have order!' (BENJY *suddenly has this idea, brightens up, then stands on table saluting line of* ACTORS *who have entered from upstage and marched around the table. They exit.* BENJY *returns to work.)*

So he left off work on what the world should look like, what sort of people, jobs and houses there should be (ACTORS *with bowler and flat cap enter, kneel at table and plead, but* BENJY *waves them away. They exit sadly.)* and turned his attention to laws. He made up laws on this... (ACTORS *enter from UL and move slowly across to exit UR holding up placards to read 'THOU SHALT NOT'.)* and laws on that... (ACTORS *enter UR and move slowly across to exit UL holding up placards to read 'THOU SHALT'.)* and laws on laws on this... (ACTORS *who held up 'THOU SHALT NOT' enter UR and hurriedly move across to UL, while those who held up 'THOU SHALT' enter UL and move across hurriedly to UR.)* and laws on laws on that... *(They cross over one another even faster.)* For the rest of the day and all through the night Benjy's pen worked faster, and faster, and faster... (ACTORS *with placards rush across from side to side, crossing over one another constantly.)* and all the time the pile of paper grew higher, and higher... (BENJY *throws screwed up paper on floor.* ACTORS *throw in more paper.)* By the time morning came (ACTORS *with laws have disappeared. One* ACTOR *appears with placard 'DAY 3'. Exits.* BENJY *yawns, stretches, rubs eyes.)* there were laws for a perfect world, and Benjy felt very pleased with himself. (BENJY *looks pleased.)*

All that day, between yawns, (BENJY *yawns)* Benjy worked on, but things became more and more difficult as the paper piled up around him. (ACTORS *throw in more paper.)* And all the time Benjy grew less and less satsified with what he'd done. (BENJY *looks glum.)* On the morning of the fourth day (ACTOR *appears with placard 'DAY 4' and exits.)* Benjy tried to look at what he'd done (BENJY *climbs onto table)* and screamed. (BENJY *screams.)*

Well, it wasn't surprising really. But things went from bad to worse. Benjy threw a fit (BENJY *tears hair, screams, jumps up and down, jumps onto floor, throws paper up.)* and the paper flew around him like a snowstorm. (BENJY *finally crumples to the ground, as final load of paper is poured over him by* ACTORS.) When it had subsided Benjy was nowhere to be found. *(This final load can come right over him.)* It was three days later (ACTOR *enters with placard 'DAY 7', then exits.)* when Sam... (SAM *apears SR.)* together with the police... (ACTOR *as policeman appears SR.)* broke in *(They break down door.)* that they found him. *(They search and eventually find him beneath the laws. Stand back amazed. They carry him out.)*

As I said, (ACTORS *all enter, forming semi-circle around table.)* Benjy was an optimist. *(They all smile knowingly.)* But then a perfect world is a little beyond anyone's creation, isn't it?

(ACTORS *all nod and exit. As* NARRATOR *closes book, he looks up at audience.)*

And yet, in the beginning, God created the heavens and the earth. And God looked at everything that he had made, and it was perfect in every way.

(NARRATOR *exits slowly.)*

There Is an Answer

CHARACTERS: NARRATOR
Seven ACTORS (or more)

(Note: Simple lighting can enhance this piece with a soft spot on the NARRATOR *and on each* ACTOR *when speaking. However, lighting is not essential. The piece is ideally suited to a sermon or talk on Jesus being the answer to our needs. Each* ACTOR's *mode of questioning and response must be different.)*

SCENE: NARRATOR *enters USR and goes to lectern DSR.* ACTORS *enter from SR and SL and take up a space in the area so that the whole area is covered. They face upstage.*

NARRATOR: *(to audience)* There are so many questions which appear to have no answers. *(Opens the Bible.)* Jesus claims to be the truth, so let us hear what he has to say in answer to our questions.

ACTOR 1: *(turning to audience sharply)* Satisfaction! That's what I want! Really deep, lasting satisfaction. *(Extends a hand.)* But how do I get hold of that?

NARRATOR: *(referring to Bible)* I am the bread of life. Whoever comes to me will never be hungry, and whoever believes in me will never be thirsty. *(*ACTOR 1 *turns back to former position, unsure, as* ACTOR 2 *turns to face audience rather more slowly and thoughtfully.)*

ACTOR 2: What worries me is the future. I want to know what lies ahead, what's going to happen tomorrow. But that's impossible. *(Head hangs down.)*

NARRATOR: I am the light of the world. Whoever follows me will not walk in darkness, but will have the light of life. *(*ACTOR 2 *looks up trying to take that in and turns upstage again as* ACTOR 3 *turns DS.)*

ACTOR 3: *(very genuinely)* I want to know the right way to live. I want my life to be a good life. But how can I be sure of that?

NARRATOR: I am the door. Everyone who comes in through me will be saved, and will find fulfilment. *(*ACTOR 3 *turns upstage pensively as* ACTOR 4 *turns DS hurriedly and fearfully.)*

ACTOR 4: I'm frightened by the vastness of life. So many questions unanswered, so many worries and fears. I want to feel secure. But how?

NARRATOR: I am the good shepherd. I know my own and my own know me. And I lay down my life for the sheep. *(*ACTOR 4 *turns upstage pensively as* ACTOR 5 *turns DS slowly as if rather shocked.)*

ACTOR 5: The fear of death. That's what scares me most. Nothing. No tomorrow. No today. Just emptiness. Is that my final destiny?

NARRATOR: I am the one who raises the dead and gives them life. Eternal life belongs to those who believe in me. *(*ACTOR 5 *turns upstage slowly and thoughtfully as* ACTOR 6 *turns DS aggressively.)*

ACTOR 6: I want to know the meaning of life. It's as simple as that. I want to know if life's puzzle has an answer, and what it is.

NARRATOR: I am the way, the truth and the life. No one can find absolute truth, except through me. *(*ACTOR 6 *turns upstage dismissively, as* ACTOR 7 *turns DS very slowly, struggling to speak.)*

ACTOR 7: But...what if I...let you down? *(The other* ACTORS *turn DS on word 'down'.)* What happens if after taking hold of all these promises I...I fail you? *(All other* ACTORS *mime 'fail you' by slowly lowering their heads into their upraised hands.)* Even deny you? *(All other* ACTORS *mime 'deny you' by suddenly lifting heads, holding out an arm and upstretched hand and turning heads away from* NARRATOR.*)* What happens then? *(All other* ACTORS *slowly lower arms and look at* NARRATOR.*)* What happens then? *(All the* ACTORS *sadly turn and start to move away, dejected, some going one way, some another.)*

NARRATOR: I will never leave you, never fail you. *(All the* ACTORS *stop and look slowly at the* NARRATOR. *The* NARRATOR *closes Bible.)* The real question is, 'Will we respond to Jesus' answers or go our own way?'

(Some of the ACTORS *move offstage, while two or three respond with a final simple movement such as partly outstretched arm and hand, a movement of the head, etc.* NARRATOR *has turned to them. Freeze. Hold for five seconds.* ACTORS *and* NARRATOR *exit.)*

Christmas Is....?

CHARACTERS: Two Newscasters; Observer; six Partygoers; four Choral speakers; five Women; four Men; two Assistants; Announcer; Child; Old lady; Father Christmas; Len; Steve; Tramp; Joseph; Mary; Passer by; two Men in inn; Matthew; two Women in inn; Wife; Revellers; three Shepherds; three Wives of shepherds; Evil figures; Jesus

N.B. Take heart! This can be done with about ten ACTORS.

Notes:

1. Don't be put off by the cast list. There is no real problem about doubling up on parts so that a smaller group can still do this piece.

2. Therefore it is quite possible for the party group to become the choral group. It just means that less props and costumes can be used, and making sure that really vital and appropriate ones are selected for

each scene. At the end, when the various tableaux are formed (if this end is followed), it will probably mean that you will have to delete the groups after FATHER CHRISTMAS.

3. Where carols are mentioned it is possible that the audience have sheets and sing them. This could be done if the atmosphere, staging, etc. was quite informal e.g. if done in a round. It would be more like a promenade performance then, and adventurous groups might like to think about this e.g. giving props and costumes to audience to hold while changing from one scene to another, making the inn scene the audience, with people in the inn dotted about the audience, while JOSEPH *and* MARY *are on the outside in the acting area. At the end therefore the lines from Isaiah could be said from within the audience by the* ACTORS, *enthusiastically, as they give out party whistles, etc. The ending could then be much more party-like, as people are encouraged to blow whistles, etc. and perhaps the* ACTORS *invite them down to the area to have a mince pie.*

4. There are various references to lighting, but if no lighting is possible, except the ordinary, then a little bit of imagination can overcome the problem! Each different scene would need to be made clear by ACTORS *entering, taking up positions, freezing, and then breaking freeze to begin. At the end of scenes* ACTORS *freeze, then exit. The choral speakers could each have a candle.*

5. The ending could be done differently, depending on preference. JESUS *does not have to appear. So long as a strong voice is heard, then visually a cross could be spotlit, or a window from behind or something that focuses the audience on the person of* JESUS. *It may be preferable to leave out all the end tableaux. Therefore the ending would mean bringing up the* NEWSCASTERS *immediately after the movement 'peel back' where the* ACTORS *would exit. The 'unto us' verses could then be highlighted by having a cross, stained glass window, or whatever, lit as the* NEWSCASTERS *fade.*

6. The news items can be made most effective by having either front or back projection of appropriate slides for each item. (Use of a duo-fade makes for a smooth flow of slides.)

SCENE: *Introductory music: 'Silent Night'—on tape or sung by audience. Superimposed over this is heard the news. Lights up on newsdesk, one on either side of the stage. 'News at Ten' music on tape.*

NEWSCASTER 1: Good evening. In Londonderry sixteen people were killed, and at least forty-five injured, some gravely, when a bomb went off in a busy department store. And in Belfast, the main shopping area has been cordoned off because of alleged bombs placed in at least a dozen stores.

NEWSCASTER 2: In London another five people have been injured through letter bombs, and two young children died when opening a Christmas parcel that contained a bomb. Police advise the public to take every precaution in examining Christmas cards and parcels, and report immediately any suspicious package.

NEWSCASTER 1: In Spain the worst prison riot for twenty-five years has occurred in Madrid. Three hundred prisoners ran riot, and there was a running battle between them and the police. Sixty-five prisoners were shot and thirteen policemen seriously injured. Three of the prison officers were brutally murdered when the authorities refused to listen to any demands.

NEWSCASTER 2: At Dagenham, Ford workers refuse to talk further about their pay claims, and at midnight tonight there will be a total closure of the plant. Following the walk out by Talbot workers in Coventry, the situation is extremely grave. It may be the start of a massive walk out as other unions follow suit.

NEWSCASTER 1: But in Great Dunmow in Essex there's one man who won't be walking out this Christmas. George Smith will be ringing the bells in the parish church from midnight tonight until midnight Christmas Day. He aims to beat the world record by at least one hour. At least the people of Great Dunmow will have a ding-dong of a Christmas!

Finally from all of us here at ITN, have a very Happy Christmas!

('Silent Night' has finally been lost as the news progresses. The sound of bells is now heard as lights fade on newsdesks. 'Ding-dong, merrily on high' can now be sung by audience—see note 3—but can be deleted. If not, lights up in hall. Then, an OBSERVER *dressed in party gear comes from the back of the*

audience. Other PARTYGOERS *appear from the back of audience after the* OBSERVER*'s lines. They blow vigorously on party whistles, etc. and then voice various comments. They are all weighed down with balloons, cans of beer, presents, food, etc., and constantly whistle, throw streamers, etc. leaving* OBSERVER *looking at them.)*

OBSERVER: *(through audience)* What is Christmas? Christmas is...what? What's it really all about?

PERSON 1: Turkey!

PERSON 2: Duck and stuffing!

PERSON 3: Beef and ham!

PERSON 4: Mince pies!

PERSON 5: Christmas pud!

PERSON 6: Trifle!

ALL: Eating too much! *(All freeze in attitude.)*

OBSERVER: But is that all? *(Group break freeze.)*

PERSON 1: Lots of beer!

PERSON 2: Sherry and wine!

PERSON 3: Whisky and brandy!

PERSON 4: Champagne!

PERSON 5: A lot of spirits!

PERSON 6: Booze and more booze!

ALL: Drinking too much! *(All freeze.)*

OBSERVER: But there must be more to it? *(Group break freeze.)*

PERSON 1: Opening presents!

PERSON 2: Cards and carol singers!

PERSON 3: Trees and stockings!

PERSON 4: Lots of telly!

PERSON 5: Pantomines and parties!

PERSON 6: Days off work!

ALL: And a right good time! *(All freeze.)*

OBSERVER: But what has all this to do with Jesus?

ALL: (*breaking freeze*) Who?

(Lights cut. Choral narration from different parts of the area.)

SPEAKER 1: And God sent the angel Gabriel to a town in Galilee called Nazareth.

SPEAKER 2: He had a message for a girl, promised in marriage to a man named Joseph.

SPEAKER 3: The girl's name was Mary. The angel came to

her and said

SPEAKER 4: Peace be with you! The Lord is with you and has greatly blessed you! Don't be afraid, Mary. You will become pregnant and give birth to a son and you will name him Jesus for he will save his people from their sins.

ALL: The people who walked in darkness have seen a great light. For unto us a child is born, unto us a son is given; and the government will be upon his shoulders, and his name will be called

SPEAKER 1: Wonderful Counsellor

SPEAKER 2: Mighty God

SPEAKER 3: Everlasting Father

SPEAKER 4: Prince of Peace.

SPEAKER 1: And the Roman Emperor Augustus sent out an order for all the people in the empire to register themselves in their home town.

SPEAKER 2: So Joseph and his wife went up to Bethlehem, in Judea.

SPEAKER 3: And while they were there the time came for Mary to have her baby.

(First verse of 'O little town of Bethlehem' played on tape or sung by audience.)

OBSERVER: *(who has been standing, listening)* So peaceful! It seems so far away now. A time of peace and goodwill! Mmm! For most of us it's last-minute rush and bustle, pushing and jostling! Here! I'll remind you!

(Lights up brightly on store scene—see note 4. There are counters with various items on sale, scarves, perfume, Christmas decorations, etc. There is some sort of Christmas music being played. People are pushing and jostling. There is a lot of noise. Different types of people ought to be portrayed, from pinstriped gent to lorry driver and youths, from overdressed, over made-up ladies, to Mrs Mop in her curlers. During this scene there is a frantic scramble to buy goods. ACTORS *not involved in specific dialogue should maintain a low level of sound, ensuring that the characters with lines can be heard.)*

WOMAN: *(at scarf counter)* Sidney! Sidney! Come over here. Sidney, I've found a lovely silk scarf. It'd go beautifully with my dress. Look... *(she turns to counter.)* Where's it gone...? *(She notices another woman with it.)* Excuse me. I wanted that scarf. I was just...

WOMAN 2: You put it down, didn't you, love! It's too late.

WOMAN 1: How dare you! Give me that back. *(She tries to snatch it.)* It's mine, do you hear! Give it to me. Sidney! Do something.

WOMAN 2: It's not yours at all! You left it, didn't yer, you stupid bag!

MAN 1: *(timidly)* Don't you speak to my wife like that or I'll...

MAN 2: Or you'll what, mate? You wanna watch it!

MAN 1: *(backing off)* Now...just a minute....You weren't even here!

MAN 2: Looking at you, mate, I didn't need to be 'ere!

ASSISTANT 1: Please! Please! What's all the trouble?

WOMAN 1: I just turned around for a moment and this woman pinched my scarf!

WOMAN 2: I never did! She left it and turned away!

WOMAN 1: That's a lie! I...

ASSISTANT 1: Please! Please! I'm sure we can find another one. If you'd just come with me we'll soon sort it out!

WOMAN 2: Aah! *(throwing scarf on the floor)* Keep yer blinkin' scarf! I hope it strangles yer! Come on, Jim!

ANNOUNCER: *(offstage on microphone)* Father Christmas on the second floor! Don't miss the grotto! The restaurant is now open for morning coffee!

(Different voices heard from all over the place amid all the general noise. But each disturbance should be the centre of interest for the audience.)

WOMAN 3: *(at another counter)* Some French perfume. What? None left? That's ridiculous!

WOMAN 4: *(at another counter)* No, twelve boxes of crackers! Well I can't help that, I need them!

ANNOUNCER: Father Christmas on the second floor! Don't miss the grotto! The restaurant is now open for morning coffee!

WOMAN 5: *(to friend)* I'll see you in the restaurant! Got to get something for Aunt Rose! Oh, a cheap scarf or something!

MAN 3: *(to child)* No, you can't have that! Get your hands

off! What? You've done what? Well, why didn't you tell me before! *(Rushes child out.)*

ASSISTANT 2: That's three pounds fifty, madam. Next please!

MAN 4: *(Enters with a huge box. He can't see, knocks into people. Angry comments.)* I'd like to exchange this please. It's too big!

ASSISTANT 2: Second floor for exchanges! Next!

MAN 4: But I bought it here!

ASSISTANT 2: Can't help that! Second floor! Next! *(He exits, knocking into people.)*

WOMAN 5: *(at scarf counter)* I'd like something rather special for my aunt, please! You see she's....

ASSISTANT 1: What colour, madam?

WOMAN 5: Well, I think she likes pink, but...

ASSISTANT 1: One pink one left at three pounds, madam. Next!

ANNOUNCER: Father Christmas on the second floor! Don't miss the grotto! The restaurant is now open for morning coffee.

OLD LADY: *(poorly dressed)* Excuse me, do you know....

WOMAN 5: *(knocking past her)* Hilda! Hilda! There you are! Wait! *(Moves off hurriedly.)*

OLD LADY: *(to assistant)* Could you tell me where....

ASSISTANT 1: *(impatiently)* What! What do you want?

OLD LADY: I wondered if you had anything for under a pound.

ASSISTANT 1: This is not a charity shop, madam! You should try Oxfam! Next please! *(All freeze.)*

(The appropriate people say the following lines in their freeze, with exaggerated venom and impatience. Then after the ANNOUNCER*'s second comment, still keeping the freeze, split everyone into two groups vocally as shown. It builds in speed and volume until it really is deafening. Then the* OBSERVER *cuts in. Alternate people can be Group 1, or one half can be Group 1, etc.)*

VOICE 1: Hope it strangles yer!

ANNOUNCER: Father Christmas on the second floor!

VOICE 2: That's ridiculous!

VOICE 3: I can't help that, I need them!

VOICE 4: No you can't have that! Get your hands off!

VOICE 5: Can't help that! Next!

ANNOUNCER: Father Christmas on the second floor!

GROUP 1: Can't help that

GROUP 2: Next!

ANNOUNCER: Father Christmas on the second floor!

GROUP 1: Can't help that!

GROUP 2: Next!

ANNOUNCER: Father Christmas on the second floor!

GROUP 1: Can't help that!

GROUP 2: Next!

ANNOUNCER: Father Christmas on the second floor!

GROUP 1: Can't help that!

GROUP 2: Next!

ANNOUNCER: Father Christmas on the second floor!

OBSERVER: *(screaming)* Happy Christmas! *(Everyone exits, taking counters, etc.)*

*(*FATHER CHRISTMAS *enters through audience, grumbling to himself, looking rather bedraggled dragging a sack. Comes onto stage.)*

FATHER CHRISTMAS: *(mimicking)* Father Christmas on the second floor! *(With feeling.)* Never again! *(Sits on a stool, takes off boot, revealing big toe through sock.)* I don't know how I got into it in the first place. It's the boss's secretary who's to blame. *(Mimics.)* 'Oh, I'm sure Cyril would do it! Such a nice man! Such a pleasant manner!' 'Well, little boy, and what do you think Father Christmas will bring you? *(Mimics little boy.)* A train set, a bike, a Kung-fu kit, a pair of boxing gloves, a kite, a walkie-talkie set, a robot, a firing tank, and a sten gun.' Is that all? Father Christmas will be weighed down, won't he! Here! Here's a magic pen! *(Mimics.)* 'Ohh! Is that all? I got one of those! Haven't you got anything else?' A clout around the ear, that's what I would have given him. Spoilt brat! And the parents are just as bad! *(Mimics.)* 'Daddy, why's Father Christmas got such a red nose?' ''Cos he's been drinkin', what d'ya think.' 'Can I go and talk to him?' 'Don't be stupid! He's only one of the shop assistants dressed up!' Shop assistant! That's what hurt me most! Me! The assistant manager!

I suppose he was right really! Dressed up for what? Nobody seems to care any more! Nobody seems to know. *(Mimics.)* 'Why do we have a Father Christmas, Mummy? What's he mean?' No answer! It's sad really, isn't it? It meant something to me you know, when I was young. It gave everything a magical air—Father Christmas, the reindeer, the rooftops and the bells. They all made Christmas the more mysterious and exciting. I can nearly feel it again now!

(Sound of bells, getting louder. Lights fade out on stage. Song—'Jingle Bells'. If this is not sung then just the bells are heard.)

*(*FATHER CHRISTMAS *is in spot at side of stage.)* Hmh! And as we get older, we seem to lose it—that magical feel, that thrill inside on Christmas Eve! We're often just as selfish, aren't we? Hmh! Peace and goodwill to all men, or only to our friends? *(Spot off.)* Happy Christmas.

(Lights up on LEN *and* STEVE *discussing a body at their feet. They are well wrapped up, holding bottles, etc. They are in fact standing in front of* STEVE*'s house. The man at their feet is some kind of tramp.)*

LEN: Don't like the look of him, you know. Reckon he should be in hospital or something—not stuck out here in the cold. Maybe we should ring for an ambulance, eh?

STEVE: (*Briskly, trying to be nonchalant.*) Nah, he's just had one too many, that's all. Come over here and have a sniff. Whisky or something... I dunno... rarely touch the stuff. *(*LEN *looks at* STEVE *in amazement. Piously.)* Police station he ought to be in, if you ask me.

LEN: Well, we can't stand here all night or he'll catch his death.... Here, Steve... couldn't you take him in for a bit? I mean, we're right on your doorstep. Just till he comes round, and then....

STEVE: *(interrupting angrily)* Oh yeah, go on, have some more good ideas. It's not much further to your house, is it? Why don't *you* take him in?

LEN: All right, keep your hair on. I only thought....

STEVE: Yes, well you can just think again, that's all. *(Getting more and more heated.)* Stupid time to dump yourself on somebody's doorstep, anyway. Mary'd do her nut. As it is I'm leaving her to do everything...filling the stockings...defrosting the turkey. Why couldn't he have picked on someone else's front gate?

LEN: Well, I don't suppose he had much choice. Here, he does look a funny colour. I'm sure he's not just drunk. *(Interrupted by church bells, or carol service noises.)* Oh help! I ought to be getting back. Promised Fran we'd go to the midnight service. Well, come on, what are we going to do with him? If you're so clever, have a good idea....

STEVE: I have. We'll move him. *(Pause.)*

LEN: Move him? Move him where?

STEVE: Oh...er...down the road. *(Getting enthusiastic.)* Yeah, down the road and put him outside old Lewis's. You can bet your life he won't be going to midnight mass. Nor filling stockings neither. Out with his fancy bit, like as not. Won't do him any harm to show a bit of charity for once in his life, will it?

LEN: *(confused and mumbling)* Yes but...it seems a bit ...well, you know...I mean, being Christmas and all that....

(Bells again.)

STEVE: Stop mumbling and give us a hand. *(They both lug the body across the stage out of sight and then return.)* There. No harm done. Well, they can't just leave him there, can they? *(Then, irritably.)* Oh, for goodness sake, Len, wish him a Happy Christmas and let's get on home or we'll be late for the service. *(STEVE disappears indoors USR.)*

LEN: *(Hesitant still and becoming despondent. Slowly.)* Yes... well...*(in direction of body)*...I *do* hope you have a Happy Christmas *(resigned)*, but it don't seem very likely to me. *(Going off.)* No, not very likely....

(Lights down. Spot on FATHER CHRISTMAS.)

FATHER CHRISTMAS: Happy Christmas! Hmh! Let's go back! Yes! Just for a bit let's go back, back to where it began! You know, Bethlehem! The shepherds! The star! Back to that magical night.

(To create atmosphere music is played, or FATHER CHRISTMAS

gets everyone to start humming 'Silent Night' before continuing.) Over the little town of Bethlehem, the stars shone brighter than ever. The people greeted each other in the streets, and all was warmth and happiness...

JOSEPH: *(interrupting at back of audience)* I wish it had been! I wish it had been like that! Forgive me, forgive me for interrupting, but you see my name is Joseph. Perhaps, it would be good for you to know what it was really like that night. Mary! *(*MARY *appears at his side. She is heavily pregnant.)* Let Mary and me recall it as best we can.

*(*MARY *and* JOSEPH *come up slowly through audience. Follow spots on them. Spot off* FATHER CHRISTMAS.*)*

MARY: It was cold, bitterly cold, as we approached Bethlehem. I was so tired I could hardly keep awake on the little donkey. I knew it wouldn't be long before the birth, but I didn't want to worry Joseph any more, so I kept praying we'd reach the town soon.

JOSEPH: It seemed so far those last few miles. We'd stumble our way to the top of one rise only to find another one in front of us. I knew with the registration we'd have difficulty finding rooms, and already it was getting dark.

MARY: About a mile away I started to get violent pains. I felt sick, tired and miserable. Why so far away from home? What would we do? I got to the point where I no longer cared, I just longed for the earth to swallow us up.

JOSEPH: And then at last we saw the lights of Bethlehem. I sensed Mary's state of despair, but knew the important thing was to get into town as soon as possible.

There were few people around when we finally got there. Most rushed past with barely a word. We had to find somewhere quickly. *(An* ACTOR *passes.)* Rooms! Are there any rooms left?

PASSER BY: Try the inn, but you'll be lucky! *(Hurries off.)*

MARY: Joseph! Joseph! Hurry!

JOSEPH: Soon now, Mary, soon!

As we turned the corner, the cold and the noise hit us at once. The wind was sharp as a knife, but the noise from the inn was warming, or so we thought. Louder and louder it got as we approached, and soon individual voices and laughter could be heard. I wasted no time in banging on the door.

(During this speech the stage is filled with people in the inn. One or two tables and stools. Mugs of wine. Dice. They start to talk, laugh, etc. which grows louder and louder. Lights up on stage as JOSEPH *bangs in mime. Nobody hears at first. Joseph bangs even louder.)*

MAN: Matthew! There's someone at the door.

MATTHEW: *(offstage)* Answer it, then! I'll be there presently.

WOMAN: Ah! Let them wait, Jonas! We'll finish the game!

*(*JOSEPH *bangs again.* MATTHEW *enters carrying jug of wine.)*

MATTHEW: All right! All right! I'm coming! Here, take the wine.

(Noise from the group.)

WIFE: *(off)* Who is it, Matthew?

MATTHEW Wait, woman, wait!

(He unbolts the door and opens it. The door can obviously be mimed at the front of the stage. He picks up lantern from a small table.)

PEOPLE: Close it, Matthew, it's cold!

MATTHEW: In time, in time! *(Holds out lantern.)* Who's there, then? Who's banging?

JOSEPH: Let us in!

MATTHEW: Who's with you?

JOSEPH: My wife and donkey. Please let us in! *(Noise from group, laughter, etc.)*

MAN 1: Come on, Matthew, shut the door, man.

WIFE: *(joining* MATTHEW*)* Who is it, Matthew, who's there?

JOSEPH: *(urgently)* In the name of God, man, let us in! My wife needs care!

WIFE: Wife! Let's look at her! *(Takes lantern.)* Where you come from?

JOSEPH: Nazareth.

MATTHEW: Nazareth, eh! Here! *(Turns to people.)* There's a couple here from Nazareth, would you believe!

MAN 2: *(laughing)* Nazareth! That little hole!

WOMAN 2: Mind you send 'em off, Matthew! No dirt in here, eh! *(All laugh.)*

WIFE: We can't help you! We're full up as it is! Coming at

this time of night! What kind of man are you?

JOSEPH: Please help us, please! We've nowhere to go and my wife is....

MATTHEW: All right! All right! We've a back room you can use. It's warm enough!

MARY: Joseph! Joseph! Please!

WIFE: What's wrong with her? We're not havin' no sick people 'ere!

JOSEPH: *(beginning to get angry)* She's pregnant, woman. If you don't help us she'll have her baby on your doorstep!

WIFE: Pregnant indeed! We'll have none of that! Matthew, lock 'em out!

WOMAN 1: Martha! Push him out and lock the door! Matthew too, if he's talking.

MARY: Help us, please! Please!

JOSEPH: On your heads be it if she dies! Can't you see we need somewhere!

WIFE: The stable, Matthew! They can have the stable and that's all! Like it or lump it! Show 'em round and close the door! Be off with you round the back! *(Pulls* MATTHEW *inside and bolts the door.)*

MATTHEW: Martha....

WIFE: That'll do 'em well enough! She's probably his whore! If she was his wife, they wouldn't be here at dead of night! Be off with yer now!

(MATTHEW *goes out at the back.)*

MAN 1: What they want, Martha?

WIFE: A couple! She's near havin' a baby, would you mind! His whore if you asks me! And then coolly asks for a room!

WOMAN 2: Packed 'em off, eh, Martha? Back to Nazareth! *(Laughter.)*

WIFE: We lent them the stable—it's mucky enough! *(Laughter.)*

MAN 2: The stable! My horse is in there! I best get it quick! *(He moves up.)*

WIFE: Quicker than that, Jonas, or you'll be a midwife!

(Laughter. MAN *2 exits. Noise and laughter continues. Lights fade on inn scene. Spot on* JOSEPH, *below stage or DSR.)*

JOSEPH: That was our reception. I was angry and ashamed!

Ashamed of how cruel people could be. I realized then why the baby had come. I remembered Mary's words, 'He will save his people from their sins.' By God they needed saving, as much as me in my anger! I heard them laughing at us, and I wanted to retaliate. Only Mary stopped me.

(During this speech the people in the inn have left, taking tables, etc. with them.)

MARY: Joseph!

JOSEPH: *(Spot follows them across front of stage and up to one side.)* We went round the back and found the stable. I remember feeling sick in my stomach as I entered. The stench, the damp, the cold, and the filth. 'Not this,' I thought. 'Dear God, not this. The baby....' Mary's hand touched my arm, and she walked past me silently, and started clearing a space.

The innkeeper came, (INNKEEPER *comes in with lantern, etc.*) and rather shamefully brought a little fresh straw. He left the lantern, muttered something, and left hurriedly. I felt sorry for him then.

We cleared a feeding trough and lined it with straw. The one or two animals nosed nearer and I had to push them away. *(Mimes this.)* I could hear the rats, and tried to forget them.

MARY: I asked Joseph to leave then. He begged not to, but I knew it would be better. For a moment or two I lay back, and it was then that I knew it would be all right. 'Don't be afraid, Mary.' I could hear the voice speaking to me. 'Don't be afraid. Don't be afraid.'

(JOSEPH *goes to one side. Spot off* MARY *and on* JOSEPH.)

JOSEPH: In the darkness outside I waited and shivered. I felt numb, not knowing what to do if anything went wrong. I could hear the voices and the laughter still, *(Laughter offstage.)* but I knew there was no real help there, neither did I want it. I looked above me at the night sky, and I knew that was where help lay. I must have been watching the stars and praying for some time, when I became aware of one star shining out much brighter than the others. It seemed as if it was moving towards me, towards this place, towards the....

MARY: Joseph! Joseph! A baby boy!

(Spot off JOSEPH. *Spot on* MARY *and* JOSEPH, *centre stage.)*

JOSEPH: *(slowly)* A baby boy. *(They look at each other.)*

JOSEPH: Jesus! *(Kneels.)*

MARY: Jesus! *(Freeze. Then break freeze.)*

JOSEPH: Mary!

MARY: It's all right, Joseph. We'll be all right now.

JOSEPH: Oh Mary! Is it true?

MARY: I don't know! I feel...Joseph, why? Why here? If....

JOSEPH: Rest now. Lie back. I'll go find help and some more blankets. Perhaps some food. Rest, rest.

(Spot off MARY. *Spot on* JOSEPH *at side. During this* WOMEN *and* SHEPHERDS *form tableau.)*

JOSEPH: I managed to get what we needed. The innkeeper and his wife actually asked if they could help. As I got to the stable, the star I'd seen before seemed to be right above me. It was then that I heard the voices and rushed in....

(Spots on MARY, WOMEN *and* SHEPHERDS, *and* JOSEPH *entering. Frozen tableaux.)*

JOSEPH: I was speechless. Around the trough were women and shepherds, kneeling, standing, praying. *(Goes to* MARY. *Break freeze.)*

SHEPHERD 1: *(excitedly)* Forgive us! This is the Christ! This baby....

SHEPHERD 2: We're not mad! We were up on the hills, trying to keep warm, when there was...there was this light....

SHEPHERD 3: All around us! And voices! We all heard them! Tonight in Bethlehem! Don't be afraid!

SHEPHERD 1: Wonderful news!

SHEPHERD 2: Yes! Yes! Your Saviour!

ALL: Christ the Lord!

JOSEPH: But...how....

SHEPHERD 3: You'll find him in a stable...

SHEPHERD 1: In a trough....

SHEPHERD 2: Here! Here!

SHEPHERD 3: There was then...well, like singing...like nothing we'd heard before! Then all became dark again, and...and we looked at each other and...and suddenly ran, and ran, and ran!

SHEPHERD 2: We fetched our wives and....

SHEPHERD 1: And we seemed to run here as if.... *(Kneels.)* This is the Saviour!

JOSEPH: Friends! My friends! *(Overcome.)*

(Moment of silence. Then one of the wives comes forward.)

WIFE 1: We must let her rest now! *(To* SHEPHERDS.*)* Out with you now! We'll come back in the morning.

WIFE 2: Have you enough food, blankets?

WIFE 3: I'll fetch some *(to* MARY.*)* I'll stay the night so you can sleep.

MARY: Thank you, all of you. I....

WIFE: Rest now. Rest. *(To* JOSEPH.*)* We'll return in the morning. Martha will stay with you when she comes back. Come all of you. *(Hustles* SHEPHERDS *out.)* Reuben! *(They exit, talking excitedly. The two* WIVES *finish tidying a little and exit.)*

JOSEPH: I pulled the blankets around Mary and went to look at the baby. Dear little child! Our baby, our...Jesus! Dear Jesus! *(Kneels. Silence. Single spotlight.)* Suddenly I felt afraid! Afraid for the child, afraid for ourselves. Afraid of what was going to happen. This little baby was all goodness. 'He will save his people from their sins.' Our baby! Our little baby! *(Laughter from offstage.)* And I felt then the force of evil against him. He was so fragile, so pure, and evil was all around, moving closer, and closer, and closer. *(Gets up.)* I couldn't stay there any longer! I had to breathe! I felt suffocated and hemmed in! *(Goes out.)*

(The laughter from offstage has become mocking. This builds up to a climax, then cuts. Single spot on MARY *and 'baby'. 'Evil motif' music.* FIGURES *in black with stockings over faces dart across stage area. A very definite sequence needs to be worked out here, which will depend on numbers. Enough people, e.g. twelve, can form a clock shape around the stage area, kneeling, and then they dart across area, exchanging places. When they have all exchanged places they slowly rise and move in on* MARY *and 'baby'. This needs to be very deliberate—*

a slow step—and as they approach, their arms are also extending outwards and upwards. FIGURES *finally tower over the spotlit area and as they descend they appear to swallow the light. Spot cuts.* MARY *exits.* JESUS *figure takes her place. Alternatively there does not have to be a* JESUS *figure, just a voice on mike offstage. See note 5 for ideas on alternative endings. As coloured lights come up on centre area, reds, greens etc.,* FIGURES *are on their knees, linked together, pulsating rhythmically, down and up. Slowly this pulsating rhythm gets quicker and quicker, out of control. They are not able to contain the force within, and on the music climax they stop on the up position. Slowly they peel back from the heads, arms losing their links, until their bodies stretch back onto the stage, and everyone has pivoted back from the waist, legs underneath. 'Good motif' music as* JESUS *emerges. White spot on him.)*

JESUS: I have come that you might know the meaning of life, and so live it to the full! I have not come to judge, but to save. You will be judged only if you do not believe me and open your heart to me. And this is the judgement—that men love darkness rather than light because their lives are self-centred. Yet the light shines in the darkness, and the darkness will never overcome it.

(FIGURES *swept out, as if by force.)*

I am the light of the world. If you believe in me you will never again walk in darkness, for you will have the light of life within you. (JESUS *goes down into audience.)*

Remember then the wonderful message of Christmas! Christ mass! Remembrance of me, remembrance of God giving himself for man! That is the true message of Christmas—God's gift of love! So remember me when you give gifts to those you love, and spare a gift for those you find difficult to love, for I came to die for all men, not just the one or two I liked the most! Christmas!

(Follow spot on JESUS. *On the stage appear different aspects of Christmas we've already seen:* OBSERVER, *store scene,* FATHER CHRISTMAS, LEN, STEVE *and the body, the inn, the* SHEPHERDS, MARY *and* JOSEPH. *Each individual or group comes onto stage area and forms a tableau in freeze of their attitude to Christmas as shown. Lights come up and down on*

each section. It gives the effect of a slide sequence.)

*(*JESUS *turns to* OBSERVER.*)* Christmas is...so much more than party hats and food and drink, as you guessed! Look to me and then all your fun and celebration will have meaning.

*(*JESUS *turns to the people in store.)* Rushing for presents you forgot, pushing and jostling, getting angry and tired—for what? For another Christmas behind you and out of the way, and just a few moments that you really enjoyed! Buy less! Rush less! Love more!

*(*JESUS *turns to* FATHER CHRISTMAS.*)* Dear Santa! If only you knew why you gave presents to everyone, and what it really is that makes Christmas so magical! Then you'd want to be Father Christmas every year!

*(*JESUS *turns to* STEVE, LEN *and the body.)* A Happy Christmas! Yet you have no thought for others. Did I come for this? Yes! Yes! This is exactly why I came. 'He will save his people from their sins.' I will—if you will come to me.

*(*JESUS *turns to people at the inn.)* I forgive you too. Even though you gave me no home. If you'd only known who you'd turned your backs on that night.

*(*JESUS *turns to shepherds.)* Dear shepherds! So confused and yet so trusting.

(Keep light on SHEPHERDS *as* MARY *and* JOSEPH *join them and freeze.)*

Dear Mary and Joseph! Thank you! With all my heart! Christmas...has come again.

*(*JESUS *exits through audience. The groups on stage re-form the stable tableau. Dim light. 'Silent Night' is heard again, broken in by the news, as previously. After a couple of items, the* NEWSCASTERS *fade in voice and light, though not completely, as these verses from Isaiah 9 are heard. These verses can either be said over the microphone offstage or on tape, or preferably by a reader. All the time the* NEWSCASTERS *become dimmer and dimmer until they fade completely by the end.)*

Unto us a child is born.
Unto us a son is given.
And the government shall be upon his shoulder.

These will be his royal titles: 'Wonderful', 'Counsellor',
'The Mighty God',
'The Everlasting Father',
'The Prince of Peace'.
His ever-expanding, peaceful government will never end.
He will rule with perfect fairness and justice from the throne of his father David.
He will bring true justice and peace to all the nations of the world.

(The 'Silent Night' carol or music is now able to take over, unlike at the beginning. Slow fade on stable tableau.)

Christmas Reading

(Note: This piece is best done within a Christmas service. It can then be followed up in the talk. Basic black costume for ACTORS, *possibly, with* MARY *and* JOSEPH *in another coloured top.* ACTORS *can come from, and return to, their seats.)*

CHARACTERS: NARRATOR
Nine ACTORS

This piece is best done within a Christmas service. It can then be followed up in the talk. Basic black costume for ACTORS, *possibly, with* MARY *and* JOSEPH *in another coloured top.* ACTORS *can come from, and return to, their seats.)*

NARRATOR: Let us listen to the word of God.
At that time, Emperor Augustus sent out an order for all the citizens of the empire to register themselves for a census. *(An* ACTOR *has slowly climbed into the pulpit and now reads from a scroll.)*

ACTOR 1: Augustus Caesar, Supreme Head of Rome, Ruler of the Empire. To all provinces of Rome, Proconsuls and Procurators. It is my imperial decree that all the world should be enrolled, and all the world taxed. All men, citizens of Rome, all people of the empire, shall go to the birthplace of their fathers and enroll in the census. I, Augustus, Supreme Head of the Roman Empire have decreed.

NARRATOR: So everyone went to register themselves, each to their own town.

(The ACTOR *comes down from the pulpit and stands in the area as census taker. Other* ACTORS *come in twos and threes from the altar area, and both side aisles. Their names are marked off. Then they all form a line across the area, upstage, with backs to the congregation.)*

Joseph went from the town of Nazareth, in Galilee, to Judea, to the town named Bethlehem, where King David was born. *(The figures of* JOSEPH *and* MARY *start slowly walking down the aisle.)* Joseph went there because he himself was a descendant of David. He went to register himself with Mary, who was promised in marriage to him. She was pregnant, and while they were in Bethlehem, the time came for her to have her baby.

*(*MARY *and* JOSEPH *should have reached the front by now and stopped. On 'baby' the* ACTORS *turn and form the inn. Two or three are 'drinking' and 'dicing' and one or two are 'serving', etc. Frozen tableau. As soon as the reader says 'son' they all come to life and freeze on the word 'inn'.)*

She gave birth to her first son, wrapped him in cloths and laid him in a manger—there was no room for them to stay in the inn. *(On 'inn'* JOSEPH *mimes knocking on the door. The innkeeper—*ACTOR 2*—breaks his freeze and comes to the door.)*

ACTOR 2: No room! *(He emphasizes this by holding up his arms as if barring* JOSEPH.*)*

JOSEPH: Please! *(Two others from the group break their freeze and come downstage similarly.)*

ACTORS 1 & 3: No room! *(Again they all emphasize their words by barring action.)*

JOSEPH: Please! *(The others break their freeze and come downstage.)*

ACTORS 4, 5, 6 & 7: No room! *(Again emphasized.)*

MARY: Please!

ALL: No room! *(Holding their freeze.)*

MARY & JOSEPH: *(turning to audience)* Please! *(Everyone is in tableau. Freeze. Then all* ACTORS *turn upstage forming a line DSC across the stage.* MARY *and* JOSEPH *also turn upstage but they are slightly downstage of the others.)*

NARRATOR: No room for *this* baby. People had made up their minds, one way or another. So many people, on that first Christmas. The innkeeper had made up his mind *(*ACTOR 2 *turns downstage as* NARRATOR *says this and then suddenly extends an arm, pointing away.)* to leave him outside. *(Freeze.)*

The revellers made up their minds *(*ACTORS 1 *&* 3 *turn downstage and then suddenly turn away, arms folded.)* to know nothing about him. *(Freeze.)*

Herod made up his mind *(*ACTOR 4 *turns downstage then swiftly raises his arm as if holding a dagger.)* to kill him. *(Freeze.)*

Joseph made up his mind *(*JOSEPH *extends his arms to surround* MARY *after turning downstage with her.)* to protect him. *(Freeze.)*

Mary made up her mind *(*MARY *holds 'baby' closer.)* to love him. *(Freeze.)*

(All ACTORS *are now frozen in attitudes.)*

Have you made up your mind about him, this Christmas? *(to audience)*

*(*ACTORS *exit after pause.)*

What Does Easter Mean to You?

CHARACTERS: REPORTER
Up to twelve ACTORS (six male and six female)

Notes:

1. Based on a true-to-life survey. Not all twelve people have to be interviewed if there are not the numbers.

2. Most of the interviewees portray 'types' of people, and it is important that each interviewee comes over as genuine.
3. The staging of this piece can be done simply—a reporter with a hand mike fixed to a portable tape recorder at his/her waist. People can be interviewed as they pass by and/or gather around to see what is going on. Of course it could just as easily be a TV reporter, with one or two acting as film crew (if you can make a mock up camera or two!).
4. Doubling up of parts is possible, but it may well make it difficult to believe in the interviewees as real people.
5. If used as part of an Easter programme it may be an idea to project the title of this sketch on to a screen above the acting area before it begins. Then different extracts of Easter music could be played, as a collage, perhaps with appropriate images projected on to the screen e.g. Easter bonnets, Easter eggs, the cross, daffodils, church, etc. If using lights, then these fade as lights come up on acting area. Then at the end the same title, images and music could be used again, perhaps interspersing the images with the title more. The piece then provides a basis for a short talk on the meaning of Easter.

REPORTER: *(with mike)* This week I've come to the High Street to ask people the question: 'What does Easter mean to you?' So let's find out shall we! *(*ACTORS *have been walking to and fro behind, some looking, some unobservant.* REPORTER *comes up to one of the passers-by.)* Excuse me. I wonder if you could tell me what Easter means to you?

WOMAN 1: Daffodils, chickens and eggs.

REPORTER: Daffodils, chickens and eggs!

WOMAN 1: Mm! Chocolate eggs! Oh, and springtime.

REPORTER: Does the cross mean anything to you then?

WOMAN 1: The cross? Now that you mention it, yes. But I wouldn't have said that.

(More ACTORS *have passed to and fro, and one or two come nearer, inquisitively.)*

REPORTER: Excuse me, sir. Does Easter mean anything to you?

MAN 1: To me? *(Pause)* Easter? *(Pause)* No. Not especially. No.

REPORTER: Do you think the cross has any relevance today?

MAN 1: Today? *(Pause)* Not as much as it used to.

REPORTER: Is it relevant to you?
MAN 1: To me? *(Pause)* Personally? *(Pause)* No.
(More people have now gathered around whispering, looking at the mike/camera, etc. See note 3.)
REPORTER: What does Good Friday mean to you, madam?
WOMAN 2: Well, that's when Jesus was crucified, wasn't it?
REPORTER: Does it make any difference to you?
WOMAN 2: Oh no. It doesn't make much difference to me.
REPORTER: Not at all?
WOMAN 2: No. No, I don't think so.
REPORTER: *(turning to another woman)* What does Easter mean to you?
WOMAN 3: *(Laughs.)*
REPORTER: Personally.
WOMAN 3: Personally? Oh I think...personally? I think it should be celebrated in the proper way. Of course, it's really for children, but I think everyone should go to church at Easter.
REPORTER: Why?
WOMAN 2: Well, the real meaning of Easter is that people should go to church, isn't it?
REPORTER: Excuse me, sir. Can you tell me what Easter means to you?
MAN 2: A few days off. You don't mean from the religious point of view do you?
REPORTER: I mean from your point of view.
MAN 2: Like I said, a few days off.
REPORTER: Does the Easter story mean anything to you?
MAN 2: I don't know really.
REPORTER: Does it have any effect on your life?
MAN 2: Oh no! It can't do really, can it? Not in this modern scientific day and age. I mean all you've got to go on is the Bible, which isn't a very good history book as many people have proved.
REPORTER: How's that?
MAN 2: Ah well, having said that, people say, 'You'll be damned,' or, 'God will strike you down,' you know. And at the back of your mind you never *really* know do you, so you sort of keep a low profile, don't you?

REPORTER: Do you go to church over Easter then?

MAN 2: Well I might. Depends on the wife. I mean it'll probably be better than usual won't it? A bit more lively than the usual boring Sunday where the choir are out of tune and the organ's overworked.

REPORTER: *(turning to someone else)* What does Easter mean to you personally? Anything? Do you ever think about it?

WOMAN 4: I know what it's about but I don't really think about it.

REPORTER: Do you ever think about Good Friday?

WOMAN 4: Was that when he died or when he rose?

REPORTER: When he died.

WOMAN 4: What's this for then?

REPORTER: We're just doing a survey to see what ordinary people think about Easter.

WOMAN 4: Well, I'm not an ordinary person. Is this on the telly/radio?

REPORTER: Yes.

WOMAN 4: Ohh! Ohh! *(She hides, laughing.)*

(Some people have drifted away, others have come up, some walk past, etc.)

REPORTER: What will this Easter mean to you?

WOMAN 5: A holiday to begin with. Yes. Um. A break certainly. And at the back of my mind I'll think of the real meaning of Easter.

REPORTER: Which is what?

WOMAN 5: Where Christ died on the cross for us, supposedly to save our souls.

REPORTER: Do you believe that?

WOMAN 5: Yes. Mmm....

REPORTER: Does it make any difference to you, to your daily life?

WOMAN 5: No, because it seems remote from my daily life.

REPORTER: Do you believe that Jesus died for you, for your selfishness?

WOMAN 5: Well, perhaps not for me personally, but for mankind.

REPORTER: But you are mankind.

WOMAN 5: Yes. Part of it.

REPORTER: Excuse me, sir, madam.... What does conversion mean to you?

MAN 3: North Sea Gas.

REPORTER: Have you read the gospel account of Easter?

MAN 3: No. I mean I find the story hard to believe—there are no facts to back it up.

WOMAN 6: I mean, things get blown up, you know....

MAN 3: Exaggerated.

WOMAN 6: Exaggerated as they go along. I mean there's no way of finding out if these stories are true, is there?

MAN 3: What I can't understand is, you get so many sightings of UFOs, photographs and the like, yet we don't believe in them, and yet we're supposed to believe that Jesus Christ died on the cross two thousand years ago to save us. Some people say Jesus Christ was a spaceman. I wouldn't say I'm an atheist, though, 'cos when I'm ill I always pray to God you know.

WOMAN 6: Oh yeah, I do. You don't have to attend church to believe. I mean you can pray at home and it still means the same.

MAN 3: I'm frightened of churches really.

REPORTER: Are you?

MAN 3: They're a bit awe inspiring, aren't they. I like walking round them, but I don't like goin' in 'em you know. I feel uncomfortable. Like starting a new job you know. You get a funny sort of feeling about the place.

WOMAN 6: I don't disbelieve and I don't believe. I'm caught in the middle you know.

REPORTER: What does this particular Easter mean to you?

MAN 4: Not a great deal. A holiday. I know it's got something to do with religion.

REPORTER: But has it for you?

MAN 4: No. Not for me.

REPORTER: Would you say that the Easter story is relevant to you?

MAN 5: No. It'll be a good holiday. Nice football matches. Nice break.

REPORTER: What do you think was the most important event in history?

MAN 5: Fulham getting to Wembley! *(Or use local big team.)*
REPORTER: Have you read the gospel account of Easter?
MAN 5: No.
REPORTER: What's going to be important to you this Easter?
MAN 6: In a religious sense? Well, nothing more than usual in the sense that Easter will be a time for a drink and a renewal of my promise to try and live nearer Christ's life, and that Christ stands for the resurrection of the flesh.
REPORTER: Do you think Easter should be relevant to others?
MAN 6: Well, yes... but it all depends on whether you believe ... whether you belong to the club!
REPORTER: Why do you think it should be relevant to others?
MAN 6: Because of the message it contains.
REPORTER: What is the message of Easter?
MAN 6: As a Christian?
REPORTER: From your point of view.
MAN 6: Well, as a Christian, it means that Christ rose from the dead and fulfilled the promise and the hope of... er... the creed that he was....
MAN 4: You've been watching one of those religious films!
MAN 6: *(agreeing)* Yes. Yes.
REPORTER: Will you actually think about what Easter means over the holiday time?
MAN 6: Oh yes. But it's my upbringing you see. Once a Catholic always a Catholic!
MAN 4: I don't think I will honestly. I'm sort of half and half.
REPORTER: Half and half?
MAN 4: Yeah. I'm a C of E Catholic.
MAN 6: It's a difficult one this is, isn't it. I mean you either sound trite or ignorant.
MAN 4: Most people are really, aren't they.
REPORTER: Do you believe the story that Jesus sweated blood in the Garden of Gethsemane out of his love for you?
MAN 4: I believe it, yeah. It's possible.
REPORTER: But it still doesn't have any effect on you?

MAN 4: It does, yeah. It means a great deal. He loved humanity.

REPORTER: The Christian would say that furthermore Jesus was flogged and beaten half to death and finally crucified for your wrongs. Should this not have some effect on your life?

MAN 4: It has an effect when I think about it, but I don't think about it very often.

REPORTER: Do you think you should think about it more?

MAN 4: Probably. Yes. But I don't. And what I can do about that I don't know. It's very difficult. I wish I could know more about it.

(Freeze. Hold for five seconds. REPORTER *then speaks into a mike and looks at audience.)*

REPORTER: What does Easter mean to you? Cut.

(If using lights cut them on the word. If not, then REPORTER *and* ACTORS *move to either side of stage area. See note 5 for follow up ending.)*

Which Side of the Cross?

CHARACTERS: NARRATOR; JESUS; PETER; JAMES; JOHN; SOLDIERS; JUDAS; TOWNS-PEOPLE; SERVANT GIRL; HIGH PRIEST; PRIESTS; MARY; MARY MAGDALENE; MARY ALPHAEUS; WITNESSES

Notes:

1. This piece can be done as a dramatic narrative by one person in a spotlight with microphone, or by a narrator (on stage or offstage) with actors onstage where suggested. The latter is how the script is presented here.

2. It is important to realize that the three 'crosses' are at the front of

the audience from the point of view of staging, i.e. above the front row, thus involving the audience physically and imaginatively, as the ACTORS *are facing the audience.*

3. The right use of sound and lighting can do much to underline the drama.

4. An effective Easter presentation is to use the script 'What Does Easter Mean to You?' before this one, using music and slides. Ideas for 'What Does Easter Mean to You?' are in the notes for that script, and here are some ideas for 'Which Side of the Cross?'

Introductory music e.g. First movement of 'Symphonia Antarctica' (Vaughan Williams) from the beginning until the line 'trickling down upon the ground'. Then it fades. A first slide sequence could occur after the phrase 'not my will but yours be done'. JESUS *figure holds a freeze, while about fifteen slides are shown, one fading in over the other. They should depict various forms of suffering e.g. a general picture, then a human face. Drums and percussion on tape could underline the slides in each case.*

A second slide sequence could occur after the phrase 'that he would accept this cup'. Again JESUS *figure freezes. This time about fifteen slides depict various forms of selfishness, again with a general picture or slogan followed by a human face e.g. Slogan of word 'greed', followed by a picture of a stock of food, followed by an emaciated face.*

A third slide sequence could occur after CAIAPHAS*' line 'Have you nothing to say in your defence?' All* ACTORS *freeze. The slide sequence needs to be made up of four or five questions, presented as slogans on walls which question God e.g. 'Why suffering?', 'Where are you God?', 'Why doesn't God care?'*

At the end of each sequence the ACTOR *or* ACTORS *break freeze and continue.*

Music might be introduced before the '8 a.m.' section e.g. excerpts from Scythian Suite by Prokofiev—2nd movement. The music cuts at the end of the 'crucify' shouts. 'Antarctica' music could be introduced over the '2 p.m.' narrated passage.

A fourth slide sequence could occur after the line 'They shrugged and went away'. ACTORS *freeze as again four or five slides are shown, slogan style, which ask questions of God e.g. 'Why doesn't God do something?' and 'Is he there?'*

A build up of drums and percussion could be used over the hostility section, 'Come down, King of Israel'. Over softer section where the group of disciples open up, excerpts from R. Strauss' 'Also Sprach Zarathustra' could be used.

A fifth slide sequence could occur on the line 'And the moment was hell'. ACTORS *freeze. About fifteen slides of those used so far e.g. slogans, faces, etc. all mixed up.*

On the blackout and over the Isaiah passage the screen could slowly become saturated with 'blood'. Various acetate slides can make this sequence up. Music over the passage could be 'Concerto de Aranjuez' by Rodrigo—2nd movement. Over the final narration, when the two Marys enter, the music could be a repeat of the softer Strauss excerpts, to keep the link between this ending and the earlier visual section of the victory of the cross.

5. These ideas are for adventurous groups, but the script does work simply so long as you have a strong NARRATOR.

6. Some groups may not be able to use the lighting ideas as suggested. It just means greater discipline! Each scene must then be introduced and concluded with freezes.

7. The dialogue by JESUS *in the first section, and by* CAIAPHAS *and* JESUS *in the '4 a.m.' section, could be spoken by the* ACTORS. *The* NARRATOR *then needs to work in with them leaving out 'he said', 'he asked', 'he pleaded', 'he cried' and 'Caiaphas recoiled'.*

8. Doubling up of parts means that the piece can be done with about ten ACTORS.

(Music is played and NARRATOR *enters DSL and goes to reading desk.)*

NARRATOR: 1 a.m. 7th April AD 30. *(Lights up dimly on* JESUS *and three* DISCIPLES.*)* Above the Temple in the little olive garden, Jesus needed their human friendship. Peter, James and John, these three, so close, he needed them. Yet at his hour of greatest need they failed him: 'I am plunged in sorrow,' he said, 'enough to break my heart.' They looked up at him sadly, exhaustion lining their features. 'Stay here and keep awake,' he pleaded. They nodded as he walked slowly away. Then flinging himself on the ground, Jesus gave way to his mortal fear: 'Father, if it is possible, take this cup from me, and yet,' as though afraid to be afraid, 'not my will but yours be done.'

(DISCIPLES *have gone to sleep.)*

The cup of suffering that was ours to bear—our lies, our pride, our selfishness laid on Jesus' head, and he was afraid.

As Jesus prayed, his anguish deepened, and he felt alone. He returned to the trio, needing their comfort, but his heart ached as he looked down at them. They were asleep.

'How can you be sleeping?' he asked. 'How can you be sleeping?' As they murmured their responses, he went back to pray.

(Keeping dim light on DISCIPLES, JESUS *is now caught in white spotlight.)*

As he knelt on the ground his body rocked as if in deep physical pain. He thought of the muscle, blood and bone to be torn from that God-given power to think, and to will. He thought of the soul that would cling to his body, until in dreadful agony, the body died. Yet this was the hard road, there was no easier way. He had come to die for mankind. 'My Father!' he cried. 'My Father!'

Rising slowly, Jesus looked back at the little group eager to lay down their lives for him. As Peter half opened his eyes, Jesus whispered across the silence, 'Simon Peter, are you too asleep? Could you not stay awake with me one hour?' Jesus sighed. 'The spirit is willing but the flesh is weak.'

This was then as true of him as of them. Yet as the weight of countless sins of men pressed upon his shoulders; he knelt to tell the Father that he would accept this cup.

(JESUS *kneels and opens himself out to heaven. Spotlight turns slowly red and* JESUS*' movements are as if he has a tremendous fever. He remains kneeling though.)*

The sweat on his forehead glistened and reddened. It ran down his face and fell on the ground. In his agony he knew it was blood. Medically it's called haematidrosis. It occurs when fear is built upon fear, suffering upon suffering. Usually the person loses consciousness. If he does not, the blood vessels expand so broadly that coming into contact with the sweat glands they burst, and the whole body sweats blood. Luke, the historian doctor later wrote, 'And his sweat became as drops of blood trickling down upon the ground.' *(The red spot fades)*

*(*JESUS *comes back to* DISCIPLES. *They slowly wake as he touches them. Music. Over music, mime betrayal scene depending on numbers i.e. two or three* SOLDIERS, *two or three* DISCIPLES, JESUS, JUDAS. *Sudden arrival of* SOLDIERS *and* JUDAS *in contrast to narration.* DISCIPLES *pull back afraid. Then slow motion sequence of* JUDAS *nearing* JESUS. *The kiss. Hold frozen tableau. Then sudden movement of soldiers to arrest* JESUS, *fleeing of* DISCIPLES. JUDAS, *face in hands, last to leave. Lights cut.)*

3. a.m. It was over. There had been little fuss. Jesus had been arrested in the garden. The disciples had fled, and Judas had got his money. He had sold the man who had promised him life everlasting.

(Bring up lights. Drumbeats. Little group around 'fire'. PETER *and others. Tableau of denial scene. Cockcrow. Break freeze.* JESUS *is marched in.* PETER *and* JESUS *look at each other, caught in two spots.* PETER *rushes out. Drumbeats build.* JESUS *pushed into centre of area by* SOLDIERS. *Lights out. Drumbeats cut.*

The narration '4. a.m. in the courtyard' to 'Peter ran from the scene' is spoken over this whole sequence.)

4. a.m. In the courtyard of the High Priest, Peter cursed and denied any knowledge of him. From somewhere far off a cock crew. Soldiers marched across the yard and halted abruptly as the prisoner stopped. Jesus looked in sorrow at the firelit face in front of him. The soldiers pushed him forward roughly, and breaking into sobs, Peter ran from the scene.

(Music. JESUS *is seen in middle of semi-circle of people as lights come up.* JESUS *faces semi-circle upstage.* CAIAPHAS *seated upstage centre.* SOLDIERS *DL and DR. Semi circle of* PRIESTS *in long black gowns. Still tableau.)*

In front of the great tribunal Jesus stood silent. Questions were fired at him from every side, but he did not answer. *(Stylized. Each* PRIEST *suddenly raising an arm and pointing at* JESUS. *One from one side and one from another.)* His face was drained of colour, and his clothes were torn and spattered with blood. His eyes were red and heavy lidded. More witnesses were called and could not agree. *(A couple of* WITNESSES *ushered in:* CAIAPHAS *snaps fingers. Mime argument as they look at* JESUS *ushered out.)*

The High Priest's case grew thinner as no one charge could be agreed upon. Rising suddenly, he pointed sternly to Jesus and said, 'Have you nothing to say in your defence?' *(Spot on* CAIAPHAS *and* JESUS.*)* Jesus said nothing and Caiaphas was caught. He could not prove the prisoner guilty of blasphemy. The court had to acquit while Jesus remained silent. In desperation, Caiaphas shouted at him: 'I command you to tell us if you are the Christ, the Son of God.'

He did not hope for an answer, for 'yes' would have meant blasphemy to them, and 'no' deception to his followers. But Jesus spoke and saved face for Caiaphas.

'I am,' *(*CAIAPHAS *recoils)* 'as you say. But I warn you, you will see me sitting at the right hand of God, and returning upon the clouds in the sky.'

CAIAPHAS: *(rising)* Blasphemy. Blasphemy! You have heard him. What is your verdict?

PRIESTS: Guilty. The prisoner is liable to death.

(The 'Guilty' cry is taken up by each of the PRIESTS *as they point their fingers of accusation at him; each one adding to the previous one's 'Guilty'. Then one of them says the final line. Most of the group converge on* JESUS, *punch, spit at him, in stylized movements.)*

NARRATOR: *(Spot off* CAIAPHAS*)*. Jesus saw the judges' anger. They rose from their seats and some came down and spat at him. He could have said, 'It is illegal to try a man at night.' He could have said, 'Without my words you would have had no case.' But he said nothing. Only Caiaphas spoke and ordered him to be well guarded until dawn. The soldiers smiled. *(Spot off* JESUS. SOLDIERS *take hold of* JESUS *roughly.)*

(Music. CAIAPHAS *comes close to* JESUS. *Signals to* SOLDIERS. *They push him out roughly. Lights out. Music fades.)*

NARRATOR: 8. a.m. Bloodied, battered and bruised, Jesus

was shoved from Jews to Romans, to Jews and back to Romans. The Roman governor, Pilate, was finally forced to do something. Weak, and frightened of his position, he gave Jesus up to be crucified. In his heart he knew he was wrong, but the cries of the crowd frightened him.

VOICES: *(As if from all around, either live or on tape.)* Crucify him, crucify him, crucify, crucify, crucify, crucify, crucify, crucify him. *(On this climax, the music too has built to a climax, and then fades.)*

(Lights up on tableau of 'Cross scene'. Two or three SOLDIERS *kneel/stand downstage centre facing audience.* JOHN, *the* MARY*'s, etc. stand huddled together slightly upstage right of them.* PRIESTS *stand upstage left of* SOLDIERS. TOWNSPEOPLE *stand centre stage. Lights grow brighter as tableau breaks freeze.* SOLDIERS *playing knucklebones, occasional coarse laughter, etc.* PRIESTS *whispering, looking up at cross.* TOWNSPEOPLE *too.* DISCIPLE *group huddled, still. Occasional look at cross.)*

NARRATOR: 2. p.m. Jesus raised himself painfully on the cross and began his final hour. For two hours it had been like this, the fight to raise himself on the cross in order to breathe, and then the unbearable pain in his feet, as the single nail pressed upward and inward. Like the other two, on either side, he fought the pain in order to breathe freely for a few moments, but the pain and the cramp and the spasms in his legs forced him to sag, until hanging by his wrists, he had to fight the pain above and battle to breathe. Jesus was nearer death than the two criminals, because he alone had also been flogged.

In front of him the High Priest and other priests, elders and townspeople mocked and sneered at him. Beneath him the soldiers played dice, drank cheap wine, laughed and swore. It was growing darker.

PRIEST 1: He said he could destroy the Temple and raise it up again in three days, but look at him. He can hardly raise himself.

PRIEST 2: Come on, Son of God, get down from the cross.

CAIAPHAS: *(sneering)* He saved others, he cannot save himself. He trusts in God, then let God deliver him, if he really is the Son of God.

SOLDIER 1: *(looking up)* Yeah, Son o' God! If you are the King of the Jews, then save yourself. *(Laughs with the others.)*

SOLDIER 2: Here! Let's toast the King: *(raises his bottle)* to the King of the Jews, to his health and happiness *(laughing)*.

SOLDIER 3: Now then! You toast us; come on! A toast! I'm talking to you! Ahh! Let's finish the game. *(Laughter subsiding. Return to game.* PRIESTS *whisper together as* CAIAPHAS *paces up and down stopping at times to look up at* JESUS.*)*

NARRATOR: It grew even darker. No thunder, no lightning, no clouds even. Many of the townspeople grew frightened and moved away. One or two came closer, wondering, waiting for... they didn't know. They shrugged and went away. *(Some* TOWNSPEOPLE *exit.)*

(Music. This might help create a mood of hostility and frustration. Lights have dimmed and colours are added here.)

CAIAPHAS: *(moving forward slowly)* Come down, King of Israel, come down. Come down, King of Israel, come down. *(Other* PRIESTS *joining in, building up the tempo.)* Come down, King of Israel, come down. Come down, come down, come down, King of Israel. Come down, come down, come down, King of Israel. *(*SOLDIERS *joining in now.)* Come down, come down, come down. *(*CAIAPHAS *and other* PRIESTS *stop.* SOLDIERS *continue.)* Down, down, down, down. *(*CROWD *make snakelike movements which build up in tempo as the* PRIESTS *and* SOLDIERS *add sharp biting movements.)*

CAIAPHAS: Admit it, you're nothing but a fraud, a deluded carpenter. Admit it, Admit it.

SOLDIERS: Fraud. Fraud. Fraud.

CAIAPHAS: *(breaking in)* Enough. We've seen how kingly he is. Let him die. *(*SOLDIERS *laugh coarsely.* CAIAPHAS *and* PRIESTS *exit. Music has faded. Coloured lights have disappeared.)*

NARRATOR: Very few people remained apart from the soldiers, and the little group of loved ones, weeping silently. Mary, his mother, and John, the only disciple who had not run away. Mary Magdalene looked up, filled with heartache for the man who had rescued her from prostitution.

The coarse laughter of the soldiers broke through the silent weeping, as Jesus' clothes were divided up among them. The crucified men moaned in pain.

SOLDIER 1: How we gonna divide this then? *(He holds up* JESUS' *tunic.)* There's no seam. *(Other* SOLDIERS *grumble.)* Well I'll have it, I found it.

SOLDIER 2: Throw for it. *(Others agree.)*

SOLDIER 1: *(snapping)* No we won't throw for it. It's mine. Mine, d'ye hear?

(They keep arguing among themselves.)

JESUS: Father, forgive them, for they don't know what they're doing.

NARRATOR: Jesus' sudden words were like a knife that cut through the quarrel, and, although half drunk, the soldiers stopped and looked up. Mary stopped weeping and moved away from John to look up at her son. His words gave the lie to the cross. They were words of forgiveness; forgiveness for the mockery of justice, for the High Priest, the Sadducees, the Pharisees, as they spat into the face of truth; forgiveness for a world which cried out for understanding, but which nailed Love to a rough wooden cross. Only a few people witnessed the presence of that love, and they were touched by it.

(Spots on JOHN , MARY *group. Music as* JOHN *looks up to* JESUS, *and slowly his arms open, his face lightens. He touches* MARY, *and she too raises her hands in wonder. She touches* MARY MAGDALENE *who again expresses openness in this moment's realization that despite the sorrow, they have come to know the love of God and will never be the same again because of this. Others in this group are opened up too.* JOHN *finally brings* MARY *forward.)*

JESUS: Mother, look, your son. *(*MARY *looks at the cross, then at* JOHN.*)* Son, your mother. *(*JOHN *takes* MARY *and leads her back.)*

(Spots fade as music fades. This music should be in total contrast to that above—peaceful, beautiful)

NARRATOR: It was not a grand farewell. As Jesus watched them walk slowly back, his eyes misted and his heart ached. He could have said much more. He could have told his mother how much he loved her, how much she had taught him, how much he understood the pain in her heart. But he knew such words would only bring greater sorrow, and so, although he longed to say more, he said nothing, but gave her another son to care and provide.

He said nothing also to the criminal who mocked him. To the other who believed in him, he promised eternal life.

(CAIAPHAS and PRIESTS return.) Caiaphas and the elders returned. They looked angrily at Jesus as they saw he was still alive—after all, the sacred Sabbath day was only a few hours away, and people would be crowding into Jerusalem. Some might even ask questions. *(CAIAPHAS whispers to PRIEST who exits.)* One of the elders went off to ask Pilate to give orders to kill these three. He was good at giving orders, and it was time Jesus was dead.

Jesus hung down on the cross, and his loved ones became a blur in front of him. He struggled to breathe and once more, pulling himself up on his wrists, he gave out a loud cry.

JESUS: Eli! Eli! Why have you deserted me!

CAIAPHAS: See! He calls for Elijah! He is calling the old prophets!

(The PRIESTS, SOLDIERS and TOWNSPEOPLE mock. The stage area is getting darker.)

NARRATOR: Jesus looked down. His cry was not to Elijah. His cry was to the Father, for at that moment Jesus' vision was darkness. The chill fear of judgement was upon him, the judgement upon the wrongs of man, every man, from creation to the end of the world lay upon him, and the moment was hell.

But the priests and elders went on mocking. *(PRIESTS and SOLDIERS and TOWNSPEOPLE jeer and make fun.)*

JESUS: It is finished! Father! Into your hands I commit my spirit!

(There is a moment's blackout, and then the stage area becomes

brighter as an explosive sound is heard.)

NARRATOR: There was a sound below ground like a stampede. Caiaphas moved back and the soldiers jumped up. The rock by which they were sitting had cracked. Down in the city, the large inner veil of the Temple was split from top to bottom. *(There is some confusion among* PRIESTS, TOWNSPEOPLE *and* SOLDIERS. *Look up at cross.* JOHN/MARY *group look at each other.* PRIEST *returns.)*

Orders came back from Pilate to kill off the condemned men and Caiaphas smiled triumphantly. He nodded to the soldiers. The soldiers moved towards Jesus. One of them said that he was dead and started to move on. Another stopped and stepped back a pace. He would make sure. *(*SOLDIER *draws back his spear and thrusts it up hard. Freeze. Blackout.)*

(In the blackout or spot NARRATOR *reads Isaiah 53:5–10 from the Living Bible.)*

He was wounded and bruised for our sins. He was chastised that we might have peace; he was lashed—and we were healed! We are the ones who strayed away like sheep. We, who left God's paths to follow our own. Yet God laid on him the guilt and sins of every one of us. He was oppressed and he was afflicted, yet he never said a word. He was brought as a lamb to the slaughter; and as a sheep before her shearers is dumb, so he stood silent before the ones condemning him. From prison and trial they led him away to his death. But who among the people of that day realized it was their sins that he was dying for—that he was suffering their punishment? He was buried like a criminal in a rich man's grave; but he had done no wrong, and had never spoken an evil word.

Yet it was the Lord's good plan to bruise him and fill him with grief. But when his soul has been made an offering for sin, then he shall have a multitude of children, many heirs. He shall live again and God's will shall prosper in his hands.

(Background music will enhance this. It needs to follow the mood—from darkness and death to triumphant victory.)

So they took his body down from the cross and laid it in a

tomb, and rolled a large stone in front of the tomb. *(ACTORS break freeze and exit.)*
(Music.) It had been a long day. A very long day. Mary of Alphaeus and Mary Magdalene sat down against the stone, not wanting to leave. Their hearts felt crushed and numbed.

(Over this the two MARYS enter and sit DSR. Faint light on them.)

To them, this was tragic defeat, as it was to the other disciples. They loved him, and in their love they missed this enormous triumph, this good news.

(Light dims on them as spot picks out a cross. ACTORS and NARRATOR exit. Hold spot on cross for some time. Then fade, as main lights come up.)

The Padded Cross

CHARACTERS: ACTOR (READER)

Notes:
This script could be used in a variety of ways.
1. As a visual aid for the reading from Mark 8:34. You could have the reading Mark 8:34–35 as an introduction, then have the drama, and conclude with the reading of Mark 8:38. The ACTOR *needs to look quite modern and enter into the area at the end of the first reading. At the end of the drama the* ACTOR *turns away and holds a freeze, while the reading is completed.*
2. As a visual aid for a sermon.
3. As a radio/tape piece, to be used in a home group or youth group situation, using readings as suggested in note 1. There can then follow discussion on 'What is a disciple?' and 'What does taking up the cross mean in everyday life?'

SCENE: *A very colourfully dressed person rushes onto the stage. The person is very energetic and conversation to the Lord is addressed to definite points above, but there's also a lot of quick reflection on the comments directed above, and these are said to himself. He exudes worldly confidence.*

ACTOR: Well! Here I am, Lord! You said 'take up your cross' and I'm here to do it. It's not easy you know, this self-denial thing. I mean to go through with it though. Yes sir! I bet you wish there were more people willing to be disciples like me! I've counted the cost, surrendered my life...it's not an easy road though, Lord, not an easy road!

Do you mind if I look over these crosses? *(The crosses are in an imaginary position behind him. He is about to look, and then immediately returns.)*

I'd like a kind of new one, Lord. I'm not fussy you understand, but a disciple has to be relevant these days. You know...nice bold colours...even multi-coloured. You haven't got one that lights up, have you? I mean my friends would go a wow on that! Quite a few conversions in that range I shouldn't doubt! Oh! and Lord...can it be comfortable? Know what I mean? Padded-vinyl or something? I'm thinking of attracting others you see, and if I could show them a comfortable one, I'm sure I could win a lot over. I mean, I'm sure my friends would go for it if they didn't notice it much. Oh! and Lord...can it sort of fold...you know...so that I can stick it under my jacket. I mean there's some people I couldn't afford to er... cross...know what I mean, Lord...could be worth my job.

Right! Now that's all that sorted out....

(He moves to look at the crosses.)

Funny! There doesn't seem to be much choice here! Just this coarse, rough wood! Are these er...end of season sales, Lord? I mean...these would hurt! No! No! These were OK two thousand years ago when people were wandering about in the desert but this is the twentieth century, Lord! 19.... *(Fill in the appropriate year.)*

I can tell you right now that none of my friends are

going to be impressed by this. I mean, they'll just think I'm a nut or something. And my family! They'll just die! They'll probably cut me off! No! No! Lord. Fair's fair. I mean, I want to be your disciple...just being with you is all that counts, but life has to have balance too. I mean, it makes that quite plain in the Bible, Lord. Still I expect you know that!

I mean, look at this cross, Lord! Nobody lives this way today! Who's going to be attracted by this! You must have something more distinctive, Lord, more eye-catching? Let's not overdo things, all right? Start getting radical like this and they'll have me off to the funny farm—know what I mean?

I mean, being a disciple is challenging and exciting and I want to do it. But I do have some rights you know!

Let's see now...colour, comfort, folding away...oh! and er...no blood OK? I can't stand the sight of blood! I don't know how you managed it, Lord, I really don't. Ugh! I don't like to think about it! Now what else is there...Lord? Lord? Jesus? Funny! Where do you suppose he went to? I don't know...strange way of getting disciples. *(He exits.)*

SECTION 3

by

Competition Finalists

A Word from the Judges

In the spring of 1984 *Buzz* magazine held a sketch-writing competition in association with Kingsway Publications. The prize for the winners was an award presented at the Greenbelt Festival and publication in this volume of sketches. The panel chosen to judge the competition were all people who work professionally in the theatre as performers, writers or script editors—Paul Burbridge, Michael Fox, Stephen and Janet Stickley, and Murray Watts. They were unanimous in choosing three outright winners and four runners-up.

First prize went to John Fewings for *Away With the Manger*. Second prize went to Stuart Todd for *And Now the News*; and Pamela Ive won third prize for *You in Your Small Corner*.

The sketches show a wide variety of style and content. Some would obviously be best suited to performance in a theatre, while others lend themselves to inclusion in a service of worship or even in a street-theatre presentation. The rules of the competition allowed each writer a free hand in choosing both the subject and the dramatic treatment, and while it is difficult for any panel to compare very diverse material, each sketch is successful in its own terms. As judges we were more interested in the way each piece was conceived and written than in what was being communicated. Many of the sketches which we rejected (and there were about 250 entries) chose very theologically laudable themes but often treated them in a wooden and undramatic manner. Structure, characterization, imagination and entertainment were high on our list of priorities. Individually the four sketches in the 'runners-up' section may seem rather idiosyncratic, but after the winners they represent the best of a whole range of work contributed to the competition.

Away with the Manger provides a neat, original idea for a Christmas presentation and will be very useful to many churches and drama groups who rely on one or two strong actors, supported by a large cast of colourfully dressed extras, children and pantomime oxen—as many of the group can muster. The increasing chaos of the action is cleverly held in check by the rhythm and rhyme of the dialogue, which strengthens the impression of trite media commercialization. It moves to a very satisfying conclusion.

And Now the News is a well-written monologue for a satirical revue. It obviously needs a competent comic actor to pull it off. Its great virtue is its topicality, but this of course is also a disadvantage in terms of publication, because it will date. So Stuart Todd's sketch is presented here as much for what it demonstrates about effective satirical writing (from which others could learn) as for its performance potential. But who knows, Torvill and Dean may still be getting sixes in their seventies?

You in Your Small Corner was one of the few pieces we received which was attempting to build genuine characters in a serious situation. So often sketches give mere cardboard cut-outs. The writing is sensitive and perceptive and its inclusion here should please actors who respond to the challenge of creating believable characters and researching the relationships behind the dialogue. The piece is almost a short play rather than a sketch and requires careful rehearsal.

The Language School tackles a subject which some might find contentious, even offensive—Christian jargon. It is well observed and the satiric target is clearly focused. Discretion will be needed in deciding when and where a sketch such as this can be performed, but by concentrating on an extreme form of jargon and exaggerating it the sketch not only exposes a certain kind of duplicity but also, by implication, deals with other problems of Christian communication. Its execution is adept, illuminating and funny.

Words of Death and Life is a good example of the way in

which language can be used to generate mood and atmosphere as well as convey meaning. Groups who regularly use 'dance-drama' and work as an ensemble will understand more instinctively how to get the best out of this kind of script. It provides the raw material for vocal and physical improvisation.

Plenty of Time is a slightly zany offering on the time-honoured theme of Noah's Ark. It should be fun to do, especially if you get the part of the Unicorn! The actor playing Noah will have to work hard not to appear pale by comparison.

The First Step Is the Biggest will appeal to those of us who enjoy dressing up and doing daft things on street corners for the sake of the kingdom! As an opener to a street theatre performance it should be effective in drawing a crowd (a couple of giant chickens outside Sainsbury's might even get arrested) as well as providing a little parable about exploring the spiritual world.

We hope that you will appreciate the efforts of all the authors here and go on to add your talents to theirs by making this material live in performance, which is the best compliment of all.

Paul Burbridge,
Michael Fox,
Stephen and Janet Stickley,
Murray Watts

Away With the Manger

By John Fewings

This sketch is particularly suited to the Christmas season, pointing out how the central character of the Nativity is often relegated to a merely supporting role. The two speaking parts (Isaacs and Bailey) represent 'the popular media'.

Suitable for a teenage-adult audience. Care should be taken to ensure that the audience/congregation is not expecting to see a typical nativity-scene, as they might be led to believe by the opening scene.

Only TWO *speaking parts have been scripted, to allow the smallest of drama groups to feel they can attempt this sketch. The supporting cast need little acting experience and could be co-opted for the occasion. Few stage directions have been given with regard to movement; intonation is slightly more important, and the timing of the rhyming is not as easy as it might first appear.*

CHARACTERS: ISAACS, *a reporter*
BAILEY, *a reporter*
Large cast of actors to mime: MARY, JOSEPH, OX, DONKEY, SHEPHERDS, SHEEP, OBSERVERS, 3 KINGS, HOST OF ANGELS, CHILDREN, SANTA CLAUS, REINDEER

SCENE: *Mary and Joseph seated on straw bales, watching over the baby Jesus. The baby is amidst straw in a free-standing, box-like manger. Little other scenery except to create 'typical nativity effect'.*

COSTUME: *As for nativity scene.*

Enter: Two reporters in modern garb, one with notepad, the other strung with camera, light meters, etc. They address the audience as much as Mary and Joseph.

ISAACS: Good evening, I'm Isaacs.

BAILEY: How d'you do? The name's Bailey.

ISAACS: From your local newspaper,

BAILEY: *The Daily Israeli*

ISAACS *(As if quoting publicity blurb)*: The people's parchment...

BAILEY *(taking up the quotation)*: with all of the news...

ISAACS: for all of the people.

BAILEY *(aside)*: That's 'all of the Jews'.

ISAACS: We heard half a rumour, and wondered if maybe ...we could make it a story.

BAILEY: With shots of the baby.

ISAACS: Might make the stop-press, we could give it a spin...

BAILEY *(musing)*: 'Late, late arrival out at the inn'—

ISAACS: A heading.

BAILEY: A picture, with your permission,

ISAACS: 'Mother and baby in stable condition'.

BAILEY: So let's keep it simple; just the kid in the shot.

ISAACS: 'The babe in the manger'. They'll love it,...a lot.

BAILEY *(he has moved to the manger to prepare for the picture being taken)*: Who's a coochy-coochy-coo?

ISAACS *(to Mary)*: Can you get it to smile?

BAILEY: Maybe... *(Hesitates over name.)*

ISAACS: ...Mary,

BAILEY: ...the mother, could sit with the child. *(Looking through camera.)*

ISAACS *(trying to help Bailey)*: Look loving,

BAILEY: Look homely ... Look down a bit. *(Focuses camera.)*

ISAACS *(helpfully)*: To the right. *(To Bailey)* Is that any better?

BAILEY *(grudgingly)*: Yeah...except for the light.

ISAACS *(noticing Joseph)*: What about you? *(Joseph mildly surprised but as compliant as Mary.)*

BAILEY: Who?

ISAACS: Joseph, the dad.

BAILEY: Stand there behind... *(Forgetting again.)*

ISAACS: Mary!

BAILEY: Look down at the lad. Now put your arm gently around your wife's shoulder.

ISAACS: Silent, but strong; that's how you'll come over. *(Noticing something behind Joseph.)* Like the ox at the back.

BAILEY *(looking up, suddenly inspired)*: Hey! We must have that creature.

ISAACS: But it's covered in muck!

BAILEY: So... we'll make it a feature.

ISAACS: Could we not clean it up?

BAILEY *(disbelieving)*: You mean, just for one shot?

ISAACS: I'd feel a lot happier. *(Moves towards back of stage, towards 'ox'.)*

BAILEY *(conceding)*: I don't see why not.

ISAACS: Say! There's even a donkey back here on the ground!

BAILEY: Could you pull it in closer?

ISAACS *(sarcastically)*: Do you want the ox to look round?

BAILEY: Looks better all the time.

(A few tentative SHEPHERDS *enter scene.)*

ISAACS: It's certainly fuller.

BAILEY: What it needs now is a touch of local colour.

ISAACS *(to Shepherds)*: Hey! What about you guys?

BAILEY: Bring the sheep, too!

ISAACS: Though it's getting to look a bit like a zoo.

BAILEY *(directing Shepherds into camera shot)*: Crouch on the floor there.

ISAACS: Mind that ox-mu(ck)... Never mind.

BAILEY *(resenting the interruption)*: Just stay kneeling right there.

ISAACS *(aside)*: Out of sight, out of mind.

(Things now begin to get a little out of hand as more and more people come on stage to be included in the shot. The pace quickens gradually.)

BAILEY: That's everybody in.

ISAACS: Except these three kings. The gifts and the robes and the crowns and the rings would just add some glamour.

BAILEY *(with abandon)*: Squeeze in at the side!

ISAACS: *(a little more cautious)*: But could we perhaps leave the camels outside?

BAILEY: Hey, Isaacs! Look up! What is it? A ghost?

ISAACS: You fool. It's an angel...and a heavenly host!

BAILEY *(to* ANGEL*: played by actor or imaginary)*: Excuse me, er...sir, could you stay there and hover? A little to the right, if it's not too much bother.

ISAACS: 'Course, we gotta have children. *(On come the* CHILDREN, *dressed in carol-singing garb, complete with olde-tyme lanterns, etc.)*

BAILEY: Singing carols,

ISAACS: lamps bobbing,

BAILEY: and Santa. *(On comes the jolly fat fellow.)*

ISAACS: And reindeer.

BAILEY: Some snow. *(Assembled company all launch handfuls of 'snow' skyward.)*

ISAACS: And a robin. *(It may be possible to rig up a slightly-larger-than-life plastic robin in flight, or something similarly incongruous.)*

*(*MARY *and* JOSEPH *are a little overpowered by it all, as are the* KINGS *and* SHEPHERDS. *The* CHILDREN *are all keen to have their pictures taken.* SANTA *is ho-ho-ho-ing. General confusion.* MARY *and* JOSEPH *almost hidden. The manger is still forward and central.)*

BAILEY: Look, I know I'm a nuisance, but it's masking the OX...Could somebody shift that dirty old box?

ISAACS *(explaining)*: Yeah, in the middle of the scene, it's a bit of a danger.

BAILEY: A fire risk!

ISAACS: A hazard!

ISAACS & BAILEY: Away with the manger!

(Two SHEPHERDS *dutifully do as they are told: the manger is removed.)*

(There is a brief pause.)

BAILEY *(looking through viewfinder)*: Good.

ISAACS *(to crowd, knowingly)*: Relax for a second.

BAILEY: Be there in a while. Now...closer together, and all at once...

ISAACS & BAILEY: Smile!

(The camera-flash goes off. No movement. No noise. A pause. The baby cries. All heads turn to look at the manger and child. Realization.)

And Now the News

by Stuart Todd

CHARACTERS: NEWSREADER
TORVILL *and* DEAN, *mimed by 2 actors (optional)*
2 *or* 3 MEN

SCENE: *A TV Studio. Chair and sign reading '10 O'Clock News'.* NEWSREADER, *smartly dressed in suit and tie etc. comes on to the set. He settles into his seat and begins to read the news.*

NEWSREADER: And now the news... *(Bangs his fist against the table.)* Dong! Massacre in Beirut. *(Bangs his fist against the table again.)* Dong! The Royal Family's Tour of the Pacific. Dong! Starvation in Brazil. *(Again bangs his fist down.)* Dong! The Big Match: England go down at Wembley. *(Rubs his fist.)* It hurts you know! And yes *(lovingly)* we have the latest on Torvill and Dean. *(Raises his arms in triumph.)* Great aren't they, eh?

But first tonight, Beirut, where Christian and Druze militia have clashed in a bloody battle in the strife-torn Lebanese capital. The carnage has left... *(*NEWSREADER *stops.)* Come on, guess. How many do you think were killed today? Five? Higher! *(His voice becomes increasingly excited.)* Ten? Higher? You can do better than that! Fifteen? Higher? Twenty? Higher! Twenty-five? Higher.

Thirty? Thirty-three actually. Never mind, viewers, better luck tomorrow. That's if anyone's left alive in Beirut tomorrow.

(The NEWSREADER *is handed a piece of paper.)*

NEWSREADER: Ah, news just in...good news. British, European, World and Olympic Ice Dance Champions, Jayne Torvill and Christopher Dean have just been awarded the MBE, CBE, OBE and have an option on the peerage. A government statement said: 'They have brought a unity to this nation when sorely needed. Five minutes on the ice with Torvill and Dean and the country's problems pale in significance.' Let's hear it for Torvill and Dean!

(The NEWSREADER *rises from his seat and begins to cheer and clap. Then sits down.)*

NEWSREADER (*joyfully*): I thank you! Next tonight, Unemployment!

(He gets up and paces right and left shouting in a monotone.)

NEWSREADER: Switch off...Switch off...Switch off. It's gone up. Big deal. I suppose you think my job's safe eh? Always news, always work? Well, you're wrong, very wrong. And you know who's to blame? *(Angrily.)* You! The viewer! You'd rather have women reading the world's woes wouldn't you? Angela Rippon...Anna Ford ...Selina Scott and that new one. You'd believe anything as long as a woman was reading it!

(He pulls out a wig from under the desk and places it on his head.)

NEWSREADER: How's that then? *(Begins to read.)* Unemployment : Hah! You'll watch now!

(He pulls the wig off.)

NEWSREADER: You're looking at a dying breed.

(A concerted Aaaaaaaa is heard from the set.)

NEWSREADER: Honestly.

(The NEWSREADER *is handed another sheet of paper.)*

NEWSREADER: Late news...Torvill and Dean are to occupy No. 10 by edict of the Queen herself, an avid supporter of Ice Dance. Earliest reports suggest that Mrs Thatcher is to coax Denis on to a rink in a desperate bid to maintain political control.

Next, the Royal Family: The Queen, Prince Philip, and The Prince and Princess of Wales are currently taking their winter break in The Pacific. Today the Queen went horse-riding, Prince Philip was on safari. Prince Charles had a game of Polo while The Princess Diana busied herself knitting for the new arrival. *(Sentimental.)* How nice eh? Just a family on holiday having fun. What could be more natural.

(He gets up, stands to attention and starts to sing the National Anthem.)

NEWSREADER: God save our gracious Queen, God save our noble Queen…happy and glorious. Long to…No! I can't go on! I can't live a lie any longer! I despise them! Yes I do! I seeth with loathing and envy. We have to freeze through another British winter while they tan themselves at the taxpayers' expense! Show me the fairness in that! I ask you? Sorry. Just a temporary aberration. It's the job. Can't understand it. I'm a loyal subject most of the time. I keep a corgi. Always watch The Queen at Christmas. Really.

(He clears his throat.)

NEWSREADER: Now to Brazil where regions of the country are suffering from severe drought and famine. In some areas rain has not fallen for three years and thousands are said to be on the verge of starvation. Gaunt-faced mothers lead their footsore, emaciated children twenty miles for drinking water. Government aid is inadequate and the international community are only now recognizing the seriousness of the problem. Swallowing hard are we? Touch of indigestion? No? Must be a good meal tonight. What is it? What are you tucking into? Cosy TV dinner? The delights of a tandoori this and vindaloo that? Beef stroganoff? Is that right? Chicken roast? *(Brief pause.)* I hope you choke on it!—Stuffing another mouth-watering spoonful into your over-exercised palates! You can't have been listening. People's stomachs are swelling up and all you can do is sit there eating your gluttonous fill! How about a helping of your treacle sponge? Go on put in an envelope and everything will be okay!

(He takes a drink of water.)

NEWSREADER: News just in: Torvill and Dean have been awarded The Nobel Peace Prize. A spokesman said it was for the couple's therapeutic influence on mankind. 'People from all over the world, having seen their performances, had recognized the aesthetic element missing from their lives and were now striving to be better people.' Wow! You heard it first on this channel.

Now sport, and tonight's big news from the big match at Wembley where England lost 1-0. Manager Bobby Robson, commenting on the disappointing result, said: 'There's a chronic shortage of world class players in England, Brian..... A chronic shortage of left-sided midfield players, Brian... A chronic shortage of wingers, Brian. A chronic shortage of your Moores' Balls' and Charltons', frankly, Brian.' *(Angrily.)* And a chronic shortage of kidney machines! Body scanners! Hospital beds and life-saving medical equipment, Brian! Put that in your game plan, Mr Robson and... I'm sorry. It's just that sometimes I get so angry I could... sorry.

(The NEWSREADER *clears his throat again and has a drink of water.)*

NEWSREADER: And finally... on a lighter note. A little tale to show you that all's well that ends well *(sarcastically)* and won't you believe it! Come on, what do you think it is? Panda bear having cubs? Derelict tower demolished? Family re-union? Miracle cure? No, none of those. Come on, guess. Of course. It's Torvill and Dean! Here in the studio!

(A cardboard figure of Torvill and Dean is brought on to the set or alternatively a-look-a-like couple who go through a dancing routine.)

NEWSREADER: They've been given the freedom by the BBC and ITV to dance Barnum and Bolero wherever they please! Take it away Jayne and Chris.

*(*TORVILL *and* DEAN *glide around the set. The* NEWSREADER *is carried away by two or three* MEN*, struggling.)*

You in Your Small Corner

by Pamela Ive

A sketch for young people and adults of the church, highlighting some of the stresses and strains that young families may have to cope with and the subsequent need for communication.

CHARACTERS: LUCY BRACKET, *Tom's wife*
TOM BRACKET
MABEL BRACKET, *Tom's mother*

These three characters are totally unaware of each other throughout the sketch. They are seen locked into their own understanding of events, talking only to the audience, and when one talks, the other two remain perfectly still, staring into the distance, apparently lost in anxious thought. It is as though they come alive only when they speak. They never so much as glance at each other, thus demonstrating the lack of communication between them. They bring considerable luggage with them and arrange most of it on the floor about them, though they may hold on to one or two items. This will ensure that appropriate gestures are not hampered and also avoid distracting the audience by dropping things.

(Enter LUCY BRACKET *pushing a pram which has an ironing-board lying across it, an over-flowing laundry basket on top of the ironing-board and an iron on top of the clothes in the basket. She is pulling a shopping trolley, obviously full of shopping. She carries a large Bible, a frying pan, a fish slice and a saucepan. She is wearing jeans and a sweater—the sort that are just out of fashion.)*

LUCY: I'm Lucy Bracket. Four years ago I married Tom. *(She smiles ecstatically.)* We could hardly wait! I was going to *share my life* with him! *(She sighs and her smile slowly fades as she looks round at all her luggage.)* But I seem to share my life with all this more than with him. If we try to talk to each other, him in there *(indicates pram)* wants feeding, or Vicky wants a story, or a game, or her potty, or the phone rings (probably his mother), or one of us has to go out, or somebody comes.

(Pauses. Looks down at her tired sweater and jeans.)

I used to wear all the latest in clothes.

(Picks up a limp strand of hair.)

My hair used to be smashing. I can't afford a perm now.

(Enter TOM BRACKET *pushing an old lawn mower. He has tied to the handles, or else he is carrying: a hoe, a spade, a tool box, a car manual, some shelves, a hammer, a brief-case, a big Bible, some children's picture books and a squash raquet.)*

TOM: I'm Tom Bracket. Four years ago I married Lucy. We could hardly wait! *(He smiles dreamily at happy memories.)* I was going to *share my life* with her! *(His smile slowly fades.)* But there's not a lot left over to share when I've seen to all this. *(He indicates his luggage.)* There's work, the house, the children, church meetings, the garden, the car, the grandparents, the squash club. It all seems to keep us apart.

(Enter MABEL BRACKET, *a smart woman in her late forties/early fifties. She carries a basket full of home-made cakes, bread, jams and marmalade etc. She also carries a telephone, some women's magazines, some knitting and a wedding album.)*

MABEL: I'm Mabel Bracket. Four years ago my Tom married Lucy. Oh they seemed so young! It was a lovely wedding!

(She smiles and sighs fondly at the memory.)

They used to pop in and see us every weekend at first. *(She adopts a very confidential tone.)* Just between you and me, I think it was a pity the children came along so soon—still, I suppose it was their choice, though... er...people do make mistakes. Course, I didn't like to ask. I wasn't told anything—just, 'Mum! You're going to be a Grandma!' I couldn't very well say, 'Have you had an accident?' could I? Lucy seems permanently worn out these days. I can't help wondering if my Tom's getting all the attention he deserves. I ask her, trying not to seem nosy, like, I say, 'What you making for supper tonight, Lucy?' She looks all surprised, like I'm talking about going to Mars. Oh she doesn't know about supper. She hasn't thought about it yet! Well! *(Shaking her head and with an expression of strong disapproval.)*

LUCY: When I was at work, I got home half an hour before Tom and started getting the supper ready. I knew where I was in those days. I could talk about work and not just children. I used to look smart. Tom works with interesting, lively people all day. And he comes home to *me*! He must think me very boring and dull. I expect that's why he doesn't talk to me very much. If he's not gone out, he's working on the car, or the garden, or the wardrobes, or he's helping someone else. Anything but sit and talk to *me*! *(Pause.)*

There's this Rita at work he mentions sometimes. Rita said this or he told Rita that. I don't know what she's like—probably an old hag full of wrinkles! *(She laughs uncertainly.)* I'm not going to let it worry me. *(She shrugs her shoulders trying to convince herself that she doesn't care.)*

TOM: Communication! That's the word these days. You have to *communicate*. Well...it's not that easy. I used to look forward to coming home from work, but Lucy doesn't seem so pleased to see me now. I hope it's because she's tired with the children, and nothing more than that. It used to be restful, coming home to her—someone who sees things the same way as you do, so you can stop battling and trying to get on with people. You should hear some of the people I have to work with! Always moaning, they are!—About everything, and bitching and ratting on each other. *(Pause.)*

I wish Lucy would give me the sort of welcome home I used to get. In the evenings, once we've got the children to bed and stopped running up and down stairs, we're pretty clapped out, and one of them usually wakes up again. We've muffled the door bell and changed to a phone that doesn't ring so loud. Most evenings, one of us is out at a meeting or something, and all the young people from the church come round on a Friday night.

MABEL: They go to church you know, my Tom and Lucy. Oh yes. But I think you can overdo that sort of thing. *(She sniffs.)* They help with the youth club. They have all these teenagers calling round, hoards of them! I think it's too much. I ring my Tom and tell him so. Well—I owe it to him, don't I? I can't just stand by and say nothing.

LUCY: Now take yesterday. Another boring walk to the library and shops. If you can call it a walk. It's more of a stop and start. Vicky has to open every garden gate that's shut and shut every open one. She wants to pick up anything lying in the gutter and stroke every dog and cat. Why sit in the pram seat when you can sit on the pavement and chew an old cigarette packet?

When Tom came in, I really wanted to talk to him. I needed a change from all that baby talk. But I was in the middle of loading the washing machine and then I couldn't leave the custard. It was just coming to the boil. I waited for Tom to come into the kitchen and give me a kiss—but all he did was sit and talk to the children! Even the dog got more attention than I did!

TOM: Now take yesterday. Terrible day at work. Old Albert's running feud with Mr Graplow came to a head. Balloon really went up! Big row—everyone taking sides. Old Albert effing and blinding non-stop all day, even started writing on the walls unmentionable things about Graplow! Dreadful atmosphere! How are you supposed to work in it? Anyway, I get home and where's Lucy? Come to meet me at the door with a big kiss? Not on your life. It's like I say, see, she doesn't want to know me. Hiding in the kitchen, she was. Far too busy for *me*. The dog gave me more of a welcome than she did. D'you think I've got BO? *(He smells his armpits.)*

MABEL: Now take yesterday. I tried to phone Tom at tea time. Well—when am I supposed to phone him? I mustn't phone when they're putting the children to bed. And I mustn't phone once they've *put* them to bed, in case I wake them up. Mind you, they still have all those teenagers going round there any time they please!—But, there, I mustn't get on my hobby horse. Anyway, there was no answer!

LUCY: Tom started his meal while I finished loading the washing machine. I'd already eaten with the children. Then Vicky toddles into the kitchen with the sauce bottle and drops it. Course, it breaks on the tiles and splatters tomato sauce everywhere! Couldn't he even stop her taking the bottle off the table? Not much to ask, is it? When I have *both* kids *all* day! Then he has to take charge of clearing up the mess, making me feel like a silly little kid and it's all *my* fault! Then the phone starts ringing and we're both determined not to answer it.

TOM: I wanted Lucy to sit down and eat with me, wanted to tell her about work. But no. She has to see to the washing! Why *now*? She's got all day for that. Vicky climbed up beside me. I didn't think to stop her taking the sauce. She's always carting things about. She takes my shoes down the garden and all that. Well, couldn't I at least eat a meal in peace? Not too much to ask, is it?—after a day like I'd had. Lucy didn't seem to think so. I should have been looking after Vicky. It was all *my* fault she dropped the sauce bottle! Anyway—she can't say I didn't help her with the clearing up!

MABEL: So I rang again. Perhaps I'd dialled the wrong number the first time. I was getting really worried, I can tell you!

LUCY: I gave Vicky her bath while Tom finished his meal. I'd already bathed Simon. Tom only had to keep an eye on him in the playpen. Perhaps he could manage that! I thought about writing Tom a letter to fix an appointment to talk to him—if he was willing of course. When I came down, the phone started ringing again. Vicky got to it before I did and cut them off, whoever it was.

MABEL: Cut off I was! Just like that! Well—I didn't know what to think. Something dreadful could have happened. George said to get the operator to try the number for me.

TOM: I took the children up to bed. Lucy said she'd make a cup of tea. I hoped we could sit down together and talk then. I had something important to tell her about work. But when I came down, Lucy was staring at the teapot, miserable as anything. Was it the wardrobes? I know I've been on them a long time. I thought I'd better get on with them and cheer her up.

LUCY: I made this cup of tea, thinking we might sit down and talk to each other, but Tom picks his up and says he's going to work on the wardrobes! I could have screamed at him! Five minutes later, he comes back and says he can't do the wardrobes. He's just remembered he promised to help Steve with his car! Said he'd have to go round to Steve's about eight. That gave us just twelve minutes to share our lives! Great!

TOM: To tell you the truth, I was glad when I remembered about helping Steve. Lucy obviously didn't want my company. I'd be best out of her way for the evening. Perhaps she'd feel better later.

MABEL: The operator rang back and said there was nothing wrong with their phone. So I tried again.

LUCY: He seemed relieved to have a reason to go out! I felt so hurt and so angry, I just blew my top—told him a few facts! That stopped him dead! Gave him quite a shock. He said he'd wanted to talk to me all the time! He was disappointed I hadn't given him a big kiss when he came in! He thought I wasn't interested in him any more!

TOM: Well, Lucy really went up the wall! Talk about fireworks! Why wouldn't I talk to her? Was she that dull? Was there someone more interesting at work? It all came pouring out. I was doing my best explaining how *I* felt when the door bell went. Three guys from the youth group with their guitars—wondered if we felt like making some music! Then Simon starts grizzling. He's cutting teeth—sore gums. Then the phone's ringing again. It's Mum. She can hear Simon crying in the background—says she'll be round straight away to help.

(He pauses.)

I wanted to tell Lucy what my boss said to me. He called me into his office, said he was pleased with me but, I ought to get this Higher National Certificate. I could do it at evening classes, two nights a week. He says *(he mimics his boss's Yorkshire accent with confidential nods.)* 'I'm not exactly *insisting*, Bracket—but I'm *strongly advising* you—you know how it is.'

(All three remain motionless, staring ahead for about five seconds then lights fade. During these closing seconds, for extra effect, the previously taped sounds of a trim phone, a door bell and a baby crying (all at once) could be played.)

The Language School

by John Beattie

CHARACTERS: THE LECTURER. *A white-coated middle-European expert*
A MALE DEMONSTRATOR
A FEMALE DEMONSTRATOR

SCENE: *A bare stage with maybe two chairs centre right for the two demonstrators. The expert* LECTURER *enters and addresses the audience—his class for the lecture.)*

LECTURER: Goot evenink. To night ve are havingk a short course in ze rudimentary elements of Kingdom language. In lesson von, ve are going to study ze syntax of 'fellowship'. To help us do zis ve are havingk two people to demonstrate ze language. Za vill have a short conversatzione, unt aftervards I vill interpret vot is the meeningk of their syaingks. First ve have ein 'Broder'.

(The MALE DEMONSTRATOR *walks on and stands where the* LECTURER *indicates.)*

Ya goot. Unt now ve have ein 'Sister'.

(*The* FEMALE DEMONSTRATOR *enters and stands where the* LECTURER *indicates near the Male Demonstrator.*)

Zo. Now za vill demonstrate to you ze language.

BROTHER (*with only a little expression, since this is a teaching demonstration*): Praise God, sister! I just want to bless you in love.

SISTER: Hallelujah!

BROTHER: The Lord has told me that I am to disciple you in the flow of Kingdom life.

SISTER: Oh! I have a real burden for body ministry.

BROTHER: So, let's fellowship in the Spirit, so that we can get on with the business of relating and share our aspirations towards situations in the local expression.

SISTER: Amen, I have peace about that.

LECTURER (*slowly*): Ya. (*Quizzically*) Goot. (*Quick shrug.*) Unt now ve vill dissect zis communicatory interaction into its component phrases, unt examine each von for its meaningk. First. (*He nods to the Male Demonstrator.*)

BROTHER: Praise God.

LECTURER: Ah. Zis is meningk 'Hello. I can't think of any better vay of openingk zis conversation.' (*He looks to the Male Demonstrator.*)

BROTHER: Sister.

LECTURER: Means—'I can't remember your name.'

BROTHER: I just want to bless you.

LECTURER: Or, 'You are not going to like zis.'

BROTHER: In love.

LECTURER: And how!

SISTER: Hallelujah.

LECTURER: Ya. Zis means, 'Hello back. I am just as spiritual as you are.'

BROTHER: The Lord has told me.

LECTURER: Zis is a complex phrase meaningk, 'How else can I get you to listen to me.'

BROTHER: That I am to disciple you.

LECTURER (*laughing*): Ya, ve have vays…

BROTHER: In the flow of Kingdom life.

LECTURER (*wistfully*): Ah, the head-long rush to be like the rest. A difficult expression to explain, coated vis overtones!

SISTER: Oh yes, I have a real burden for body ministry.

LECTURER: Ah, getting ze other body to do the vork, or passing ze berk.

BROTHER: So let's fellowship.

LECTURER: Ya, a fun little phrase meaningk, 'chat'. As in 'avachat'.

BROTHER: In the Spirit.

LECTURER: A little semantic device to save praying.

BROTHER: So that we can get on with the business of relating.

LECTURER: I zink zis is some sort of code for friendship, I zink.

BROTHER: And share our aspirations

LECTURER *(laughing)*: I zink zis not the sharing of the headache pills, no, ya?

BROTHER: towards situations.

LECTURER: Maybe zis is a euphemism for ze problem. Change ze name unt it goes away, ya? No.

BROTHER: In the local expression.

LECTURER *(quizzically)*: Ze church? Is zis a language, or is zis a language!

SISTER: Amen.

LECTURER: Zis is a very interesting portmanteau vord vis many meaningks. 'I hope zis is ze end of ze conversation', or 'Zere is no answer to zat', or even 'I didn't understand a vord you said'.

SISTER: I've got peace about that.

LECTURER: Ya, Ya, it doesn't bother me, boyo, either. *(Pause.)*

Unt so ve conclude our lesson, I'm sure it hasn't bothered you either. Gooten acht.

(Bows deeply. Exit all three.)

Words of Death and Life

by Roland Heaney

Christian drama often consists of retelling stories or parables, providing entertainment or offering a challenge to its hearers.

The aims of this sketch are somewhat different. It was written in the hope that it would produce an act of worship with which its audience could identify. Possibly the most suitable setting for the sketch is in a church, to either a teenage or adult audience.

The subject of the sketch, the death and resurrection of Jesus Christ, is central to the Christian faith. Looking back on the completed events, it is easy for us to forget how traumatic those experiences must have been for the followers of Jesus at that time. This sketch tries to capture the mood of those events for the followers.

*The sketch is written for three characters (*A, B, *and* C*) who express themselves with voice and mime. Characters should be uniformly dressed in simple costume.*

As the stage area of many ecclesiastical buildings is limited (with poor visibility for the audience), movement within the sketch can be kept to a minimum.

*The sketch begins with the three characters (*A, B, *and* C*) facing away from the audience;* B *is positioned central stage with* A *and* C *on either side.*

A: Garden *(Turning to audience.)*
B: Garden *(Turning to audience.)*
C: Garden *(Turning to audience.)*
A: Garden
B: Garden
(Slow, even, rhythm with little movement.)
C: Cold

A: Garden
B: Dark
C: Dark
A: Garden
B: Lonely
C: Garden
A: Garden
B: Listen
C: Garden
A: Listen
B: Listen
C: Listen

(Excitement and fear. Increase in tempo and crescendo with appropriate actions.)

A: They are coming
B: Watch
C: Listen
A: Listen
B: Watch
C: They are coming
A: They are coming
B: Listen
C: They are coming
A: Coming
B: Coming
C: Arrest him
A: Coming
B: They are here
C: Arrest him
A: Arrest him
C: Arrest him
A: Arrest him
C: Seize him

*(*A *and* C *seize hold of* B*)*

A and C: Arrest him
A and C: Arrest him
A and C: Arrest him
A and C: Arrest him *(Climax.)*

*(*A *and* B *leave stage;* A *forcefully pulling* B *off.* C *moves to*

middle of stage facing audience.)
(Trial slow even rhythm throughout. Volume—low gradually increasing to maximum with Golgotha. C *mimes action finishing in crucifix position.)*

A and B *(offstage)*: Try him
Try him
Try him
Try him
Try him
Beat him
Try him
Try him
Try him
Beat him
Beat him
Try him
Beat him
Beat him
Beat him
Beat him
Beat him
Beat him
Kill him
Beat him
Beat him
Kill him
Kill him
Kill him
Kill him
Kill him
Kill him
Crucify him
Crucify him
Crucify him
Crucify him
Crucify him
Crucify him

(Climax, audible whisper.)

Golgotha

Crucify him
Crucify him

(Pause for approximately ten seconds, C *returns to normal standing position facing audience.)*

C: He was oppressed, and he was afflicted, yet he opened not his mouth: like a lamb that is led to the slaughter, and like a sheep before its shearers is dumb, so he opened not his mouth.

(Pause for approximately ten seconds, C *slowly moves from centre of stage to original position.)*

B *(enters walking slowly with head bowed to centre stage and facing audience.)*: Jesus is dead.

A *(enters walking slowly with head bowed to original position and facing audience)*: Jesus is dead.

(Mourning. Very slow rhythm. Quiet.)

C: Dead
A: Dead
B: Dead
C: Jesus is dead
A: Dead
B: Dead
C: Dead
A: Destruction
B: Death
C: Death
A: Despair
B: Death
C: The End
A: Death
B: Death
C: Death
A: Sorrow
B: Death
C: Death
A: What
B: Death
C: Death
A: When
B: Death

C: Death
A: Listen
B: Death
(Unbelief changing to hope. Increase in tempo and crescendo.)
C: Listen
A: News
B: News
C: What
A: Listen
B: News
C: Listen
A: No
B: Risen
C: Risen
A: No
B: Risen
C: Risen
A: Risen
B: News
C: Risen
A: When
B: Risen
C: Risen
A: Alive
B: Risen
C: Risen
A: Alive
B: Hope
C: Alive
A: Alive
B: Hope
C: Joy
(Excitement.)
A: Alive
B: Alive
C: Alive
A: Look *(Pointing towards imaginary figure.)*
B: Alive
C: Look

A: Look
B: Alive
C: Look
A: Shore
B: Look
C: Shore
A: Standing
B: Shore
C: Look
A: Waiting
B: Waiting
C: Look
A: Waiting
B: It is him *(Recognition and wonder.)*
C: It is him
A: Waiting
B: It is him
C: It is him
A: It is him
B: It is him
C: It is Jesus
A: It is him
B: It is him
(Climax—with emphasis on 'is'.)
C: It is Jesus
(Pause.)
(Worship. Quiet.)
A: Jesus
B: It is Jesus
C: Jesus
A: Jesus
B: Alive
C: Jesus
A: Lord
B: Jesus
C: Jesus
(Gradual increase in tempo and crescendo to reach maximum for finale.)
A: Lord

B: Lord
C: Lord
A: Jesus
B: Lord
C: King
A: King
B: Lord
C: King
A: King
B: King
C: Saviour
A: King
B: King
C: Saviour
A: Saviour
B: King
C: Saviour
A B and C: Lord!

(Climax. A *and* C *kneel down with raised hands.* B *remains standing with raised hands position held for approximately ten seconds.)*

Plenty of Time

by Graeme Kent

CHARACTERS: NOAH
UNICORN

SCENE: *The curtain rises on a set depicting a cave. There are pictures on the walls, furniture scattered about the floor. A* UNICORN *is sleeping contentedly in an armchair. He is lazy, self-satisfied, not very bright.*

(Depending upon the character of the production, the Unicorn

could either be wearing a solitary cardboard horn, or a more elaborate costume. Similarly, his movements could be prosaic or, in a more professional production, involve an element of mime or ballet.)

There is a knock at the door. The UNICORN *wakes up. The knock is repeated. Reluctantly the unicorn rises, walks over and opens the door.* NOAH *is standing outside in flowing robes. He is old, dignified, conscientious, but impatient and easily irritated.*

NOAH: Mr Unicorn?

UNICORN: Not today, thank you.

(He closes the door and shambles back to his chair. The knock is repeated. Reluctantly the UNICORN *goes back and opens the door again.)*

UNICORN: I'm sorry. I never buy anything at the door.

NOAH: I'm not a salesman. I'm Noah. Perhaps you've heard of me.

UNICORN: No, I don't think so. Good night.

(He tries to shut the door. NOAH *steps forward, forestalling him.)*

NOAH: You must have heard of me! I'm Noah. You know, I'm building the ark on the top of that mountain over there.

UNICORN: Oh, batty Noah! *(Confused.)* I'm sorry, I didn't mean—

NOAH: I believe you're one of my neighbours who signed a petition complaining about the noise I've been making.

UNICORN: Well, I suppose you realise what you've done to property values in this area. All these wild parties you've been throwing. People coming and going at all hours of the night and day. Bit anti-social, you know.

NOAH: I haven't been giving parties. I'm trying to save the world!

UNICORN: You're not a Jehovah's Witness, are you?

NOAH: No, I am not! Look, may I come in just for a moment? This really is important.

UNICORN: I suppose so.

*(*NOAH *comes in. The* UNICORN *closes the door and comes back and slumps into his chair.* NOAH *paces impatiently up and down.)*

UNICORN: I can only spare a few minutes. You can see how busy I am.

NOAH: I certainly can. Very well, I'll come straight to the point. I'm here to offer you and Mrs Unicorn a place on my ark.

UNICORN: You what?

NOAH: I'm afraid I must ask you to hurry. It's just started to rain, just as he prophesied. That means we've only got forty days left. I've got to round up the rest of the animals quickly.

UNICORN: Now just a minute, squire. Hang about. You've lost me. Off on some sort of cruise are you?

NOAH: Off on a cruise? Haven't you heard?

UNICORN: Heard what? We don't get out very much. Homebodies, you could call us.

NOAH: The Lord God himself spoke to me.

UNICORN: Oh yes? That's nice.

NOAH: The Lord said: 'Make thee an ark of gopher wood; Rooms shalt thou make in the ark, and shalt pitch it within and without with pitch.'

UNICORN: Really? I believe this do-it-yourself is all the rage in some circles. Sort of a hobby, this woodwork, is it?

NOAH: No, it is not a hobby! Don't you understand? The world is coming to an end!

UNICORN: But I haven't had my holidays yet.

NOAH: This is no time to be thinking about holidays! I'm offering you a chance to save your life and propagate your species!

UNICORN: Language! Language!

NOAH: I'm sorry. How can I make you understand. Look I'll tell you what the Lord said. Are you ready?

UNICORN: Fire away, chief.

NOAH: Right. These are his exact words, mind.

UNICORN: I'm with you.

NOAH: The Lord God said, 'And, behold I, even I, do bring a flood of waters upon the earth, to destroy all flesh, wherein is the breath of life, from under heaven; and every thing that is in the earth shall die.'

UNICORN: Bit drastic, isn't it?

NOAH: Will you listen! And the Lord God said unto me: 'But with thee will I establish my covenant; and thou shalt come into the ark, thou, and thy sons, and thy wife, and thy sons' wives with thee.'

UNICORN: Sort of family outing, like.

NOAH: There's more! 'And of every living thing of all flesh, two of every sort shalt thou bring into the ark, to keep them alive with thee; they shall be male and female. Of fowls after their kind, and of cattle after their kind, of every creeping thing of the earth after his kind, two of every sort shall come unto thee, to keep them alive.' There, now do you understand?

UNICORN *(pause)*: No.

NOAH *(his self-possession going)*: You stupid animal! The world is coming to an end! I've got to get two of every kind of bird and beast on board the ark and sale within the week. I've got most of them rounded up, but you and some of your thick friends are ignoring the situation!

UNICORN: No need to be offensive, you know.

NOAH: I'm sorry.

UNICORN: If you can't debate a subject rationally, then your case can't be very strong.

NOAH: Forgive me, I shouldn't have lost my temper. I've been overworking lately.

UNICORN *(drowsily)*: We all do that, squire.

NOAH: Yes, I suppose so.

(The UNICORN *rises. He is cool, thinking himself very much in command of the situation.)*

UNICORN: Right, we'll just examine the situation, shall we?

NOAH *(breathing hard)*: If you must.

UNICORN: All right. You're going to take two of every kind of bird and beast with you—right?

NOAH *(controlling himself)*: That is my intention, yes.

UNICORN: All right then, John, tell me this. Just how big is this ark of yours?

NOAH: The Lord gave me the exact measurements. 'The length of the ark shall be three hundred cubits, the breadth of it fifty cubits, and the height of it thirty cubits.'

UNICORN: Three hundred by fifty by thirty? To house every

living creature on earth?

NOAH: Two of each kind, yes.

UNICORN *(triumphantly)*: Well then, you're never going to do it. You'll be overcrowded. The health and safety authorities will do you.

NOAH: When the world comes to an end there won't be any health and safety authorities.

UNICORN: That's what you think. I won't ask you about the health and sanitation arrangements on board, but tell me this—how are you going to feed all those creatures?

NOAH: We shall take supplies of food with us on the voyage.

UNICORN: Enough to feed the birds of the air and the beasts of the field and the creepy-crawlies? Do me a favour. And tell me this. Where are you building this ark of yours?

NOAH: You know very well—on the top of the mountain.

UNICORN: Exactly. Allow me to bring one other fact to your attention. You're nowhere near the sea. How are you going to launch the ark?

NOAH: The world is going to be covered with water, the rain will come down for forty days and forty nights. When the level rises high enough the ark will just float off.

UNICORN: Pull the other one, this one's got bells on it. *(Pause.)* You're serious, aren't you? You think the ark is just going to float off the top of a mountain. Mr Noah, may I ask you a personal question? How old are you?

NOAH: I don't see what—

UNICORN: No, come on, how old are you?

NOAH: If you must know, I'm... *(mutters)* six hundred.

UNICORN: How old?

NOAH *(defiantly)*: Six hundred!

UNICORN: Stroll on!

NOAH: What's wrong with being six hundred?

UNICORN: With respect, it's hardly the first flush of youth, is it?

NOAH: What are you trying to say?

UNICORN: Well, look at it from my point of view. A six hundred year old geriatric hears voices, builds himself a ramshackle boat kilometres from the nearest water, with no professional help, crams it full of all kinds of animals, most of whom hate the sight of each other, with totally inadequate messing and sanitary facilities, and then he tries to persuade me and my lady wife to go with him! You'll pardon me if I say I've had better offers.

NOAH: I know it all sounds unusual—

UNICORN: Unusual? It's all about as likely as a straight banana! Do you know what I think, sunshine?

NOAH: No, but I'm sure you're going to tell me.

UNICORN: I think you *are* trying to sell me something. You've gone into the travel agency business. This spiel about hearing voices is all a con. You're trying to flog tickets for a sea-trip. You can't fool me, mate.

NOAH *(through clenched teeth)*: You stubborn, conceited ignorant know-all—

UNICORN: Oh, charming. We're seeing the real you now, aren't we? You couldn't fool me with your sales-patter, so now you're descending to vulgar abuse. Typical! I've met your sort before. Cave-to-cave salesman.

NOAH: For the last time, are you going to take this chance to save your life and preserve your species?

UNICORN *(loftily)*: If it's all the same to you, squire, I'll pass this time. On the whole, I think my good lady and I prefer Benidorm.

NOAH: You know what this means, don't you? It will mean the end of the unicorns on earth.

UNICORN: Do you reckon? I'll take my chances. Believe me, we'll be around for a few million years yet.

NOAH: I can't waste any more time on you. I've got more animals to collect.

UNICORN: Oh yes? Who's that then?

NOAH *(produces list and consults it)*: The dragon, the dodo, the phoenix, and the gryphon.

UNICORN: You can forget about that lot for a start! They'll never come with you. Very sensible bunch they are. They won't go on any wild trip.

NOAH: Then like you, their days are numbered.

UNICORN: If you believe that, you'll believe anything.

NOAH: You won't reconsider?

UNICORN: Why should I?

NOAH: It's all a matter of faith.

UNICORN: What's that when it's at home?

NOAH: Goodbye, unicorn. I really am very sorry.

UNICORN: That's all right, Noah. I'll live with it.

(Sadly NOAH *goes out, closing the door behind him. The* UNICORN *sits down with relief.)*

UNICORN: Funny fellow. There are some real weirdos around these days.

(Bring up rain falling heavily outside.)

Listen to that rain. I'd better go out and check the roof some time. Not yet though. There's plenty of time... I know when I'm well off!

(His head falls back. Soon he is snoring loudly.)

The First Step Is the Biggest

by Adrian Self

CHARACTERS: BIRD 1
BIRD 2

This sketch is written for young teenagers upward, for a church or a secular audience.

SCENE: *The stage is empty. On walk two people dressed as birds.*

BIRD 1: So Donald said, 'Why would you go mad if you flew, of all things, upside down?' So I said, 'I don't know. Why?' And he said, 'Because you would be quacking up'. Get it? Look, a duck quacks, right? So if it was upside down it would quack up, okay?

BIRD 2: But you're not a duck you're a seagull.

BIRD 1: Yes, well, the principle's the same. Anyway, what are we going to do today?

BIRD 2: Today you're going to learn how to fly.

BIRD 1: Eh? Oh, I see, yes, very funny. Not quite as good as Donald's, but not bad.

BIRD 2: I'm serious. Today you are going to fly.

BIRD 1: Look, that's all right for you, you want to fly, all well and good. But for me, well, it's just not natural, is it? Anyway, I'm happy in my roof garden. This is where I was born and this is where I'll stay. You want to fly, then go ahead. I'll not mock you with your funny ideas. Just leave me here, all right?

BIRD 2: But you don't know what you're missing; and it's the most natural thing in the world.

BIRD 1: Listen. If we were meant to fly we would have been given propellers. Anyway, I do all the so-called right things. *(Illustrates.)* Flapping the wings, running a bit, maybe even jumping in the air every now and then. It does nothing for me.

BIRD 2: That's because you're not actually flying, are you?

BIRD 1: Well no, not actually flying. But it's not far from it.

BIRD 2: Yes it is. You can't possibly know what it's like because you refuse to try the real thing. So you can never find out how wonderful it is.

BIRD 1: Look, you say I've never tried the real thing, as you call it. Well, okay. How do you go about it?

BIRD 2: It's very simple. All you have to do is really want to. Now, are you sure you really want to?

BIRD 1: Nn...yes.

BIRD 2: Good. Now walk up to the edge here, that's right. Yes, I know it looks a long way down. Now flap your wings. No, no...not quite like that. Yes, you're really getting the hang of it now. Now all you have to do is jump off.

BIRD 1: Are you crazy! Have you seen the drop? Who do you think you are, Birdbrain?

BIRD 2: Listen, you haven't done this before. To you it may

look crazy. But all you need to do is have faith and try it. You've seen other birds do it, so what's the problem?

BIRD 1: It's all very well you saying that; you're good enough to do it, but me, well, I don't think I am.

BIRD 2: You're good enough. You were born to fly.

BIRD 1: Yes, but I don't know if I can. I mean, I don't really understand what it's all about.

BIRD 2: Look, you don't have to understand it all, you'll learn more as you practise. All you have to do is take the first step.

BIRD 1: Bird, that is a big step.

BIRD 2: Yes, but it's the step that will make all the difference. The difference between existing and really living. Look at you, you're tied down here, you're going nowhere. This can set you free to live life to the full, and anyway, you can't outrun that cat for ever, this can put you out of his reach. *(*BIRD 2 *flies off stage.* BIRD 1 *runs after him.)*

Back to Back's Little Black Paperback Book

by Fraser Grace

How do you do drama?
Why should you do it?
Who can you do it to, and why do they deserve it?

At last, the answers to these questions, and many more, are brought to you in glorious black and white. Whether you prefer to write the script or take the leading role on the night of the big performance, Back to Back guide you through the world of drama in evangelism.

Join them now in the quest for The 100% Foolproof Blueprint for Brilliant Sketches Every Time.

Read examples of their work.

It's all there—so don't miss Back to Back's Little Black Paperback Book.

You *know* it makes sense.